# Michael Avon OEMING
## On His Work and Career

A Conversation with
**Bill Baker**

ROSEN
PUBLISHING®

New York

Published in 2008 by The Rosen Publishing Group, Inc.
29 East 21st Street, New York, NY 10010

An abbreviated version of "Michael Avon Oeming: The Comeback Kid"
appeared in *Comics Explorer* Vol. 1, No. 1, Issue 1, November 2002.

First Edition

**Library of Congress Cataloging-in-Publication Data**

Oeming, Michael Avon.
Michael Avon Oeming on his work and career / [interviewer], Bill
Baker. — 1st ed.
    p. cm. — (Talking with graphic novelists)
Includes bibliographical references and index.
ISBN-13: 978-1-4042-1075-2
ISBN-10: 1-4042-1075-X
1. Oeming, Michael Avon—Interviews. I. Baker, Bill, 1958– II. Title.
PN6727.O39Z46 2008
741.5'092—dc22

                                                              2007000939

*Manufactured in the United States of America*

Cover photo of Michael Avon Oeming © 2007 Bill Baker.

# Table of Contents

# *Interview*

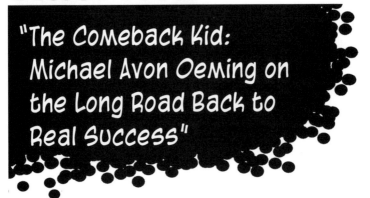

"The Comeback Kid:
Michael Avon Oeming on
the Long Road Back to
Real Success"

To an outside observer, it might seem a given that Michael Avon Oeming has led a charmed life. As with most things in this world, appearances and assumptions can be deceiving. The reality is that, like all of us, this highly accomplished creator has had his own obstacles to surmount and circumvent over the years. In fact, it might have been his first brush with "big time" success that led to him facing perhaps his darkest moment.

It's no small wonder if anyone can remember when a very, very young lad named Mike Oeming, protégé of Adam Hughes and Neil Vokes, left his adoptive home in Texas seeking fame and fortune creating comics. Soon he was drawing Judge Dredd for DC Comics and seemed to have made it in the "big leagues." Still, it's a rare thing when all goes as planned, and this particular artist's journey proved to be no exception. Despite all of his best efforts at the time, he eventually found himself without steady employment in his chosen field. With a family to help support, he did the only thing he could—he got a "real" job.

And then, a truly amazing thing happened.

But perhaps it'd be best if Oeming told the tale of how he suddenly, unexpectedly found himself back on the road to four-color glory alongside the likes of Brian Bendis and Mark Wheatley, and how he plans to walk that road in the future.

**Bill Baker:** *You're just sitting around doing a whole lot of nothing these days, right?*

**Mike Oeming:** [*laughter*] Pretty much. Just twiddling my thumbs, you know.

**BB:** *Seriously, you're incredibly busy these days. Why don't you give us a rundown on the different projects you're working on?*

**MO:** Well, obviously *Powers*. It's a monthly book, and I'm just trying to stay on top of that schedule. Which started out fine, and then I fell behind a little, work-wise, when I took on some of the other projects which started out fine, but then schedules kind of collided. Then there was some personal family stuff that slowed things down, too, as soon as I started catching up on that. So, just now, I'm finally starting to get regular with the book, where it's fully monthly again, versus say every six weeks, or six to eight weeks it was shipping. In fact, we're hoping that next year we can even start double shipping on issues. That I'll be far enough ahead that we can actually get, say for 2003, get like fifteen to sixteen issues out. That's what we'd really like to do, is kind of catch up a bit.

Right now, obviously besides *Powers*, the only other thing I'm actively working on is the next *Hammer of the Gods* miniseries, which will be coming out through Image in color. The trade's coming out in color, that's a [collection] of the original black-and-white miniseries that we originally did through Insight [Studios], and that'll be out in a color trade in September, and then January starts the new miniseries.

And I just finished up the last issue of *Bastard Samurai* with Kelsey Shannon. So, right now, those are the only things I'm really hard-core, actively working on. But I've got several other projects that I'm working on, kind of on the side, as they develop. I've written a couple of scripts, like one-shot deals, that other people are drawing. So I'm going to be doing several projects that I'm only writing, and not drawing. But next year, after *Hammer of the Gods*, then I do have two other miniseries that I'll be writing and drawing myself.

**BB:** *What can you tell us about the new stuff?*

**MO:** The stuff that I'll be working on myself, the first one will be out right after the *Hammer of the Gods* mini. That one's created by myself, and written and cocreated by Christopher Golden, who writes for *Hellboy* and *Buffy* [*the Vampire Slayer*] novels.

**BB:** *Right. He's also won awards and a lot of critical praise for his own horror novels, too.*

**MO:** Yeah. He's been nominated for [numerous awards for his] science fiction and horror novels and stuff. And he's a really fun writer, and he's a really nice guy. We get along really well. So I had an idea that I thought he'd be perfect for. It's a three-issue miniseries called *Nevermore*. Most likely Image will do it, because they seem to like me. [*general laughter*] They seem to let me do whatever I want. And I'll start that after the next *Hammer*, as long as my *Powers* is on schedule. That's kind of my basic rule of thumb, it's I can go ahead and do whatever I want to do, as long as *Powers* is shipping on time. And, like I said, we plan on getting ahead of schedule, which I'm kind of in the middle of right now. Actually getting a good six issues ahead.

So the *Nevermore* series will probably be in color. I'm penciling, inking myself, cowriting it with Chris, and it's a lot of fun. It will be my first all-ages book, I think.

**BB:** *Can you give us an idea of what the basic premise and plot is?*

**MO:** Not so much the plot, but, basically, the story kind of gestated from watching [a film]. I got my son the *Yellow Submarine*, the Beatles film, which we just absolutely loved, and I was just watching it and there's a lot of imagery and stuff that got me thinking. I had been into the Beatles for a long time, and I'd always liked the Beatles cartoon, and the *Scooby-Doo* cartoon, and my son loves the *Scooby-Doo* cartoon, the original. We just love watching it together. So I kind of came up with this idea that's kind of an amalgamation between a couple of different things that I really liked, which is Edgar Allan Poe, the Beatles, and *Scooby-Doo.* [*laughter*]

So it's about this Goth Poe band that travels around the country solving mysteries that are based on magic and evil and stuff like that. There are four characters that, originally, they were all Beatles-based characters. But just to get away from lawsuits, I decided to say, "Well, since I've already got the Poe thing, let me make them Poe-based characters." So each one of the characters have a Poe-based super power.

For instance, the John Lennon-like character, I think we're calling him the Raven. Originally, I was going to call him Blackbird, but that was going to be based on Paul McCartney's song. But we decided Paul was going to be like this sort of cat character. Again, it's not really Paul and John. John's the only one that's really kind of left over from the Beatles phase of it. So John is the Raven character, and he's got wings and he can kind of control other birds, and he's got these unique claws and stuff. It's very quirky and very fun. Very character- and design-based. And the Masque of the Red Death shows up; of course he's our main villain.

And they travel around in a Winnebago, and solve mysteries. They get their orders from the All Seeing Eye, which is another Poe theme. We carry a lot of Poe themes into the book. And we're trying to do Poe stuff that hasn't been done, because there's a lot of Poe comics. So we're very aware of the other Poe comics, and being respectful of both them and the source material, to not bump heads with other creators. So we're definitely doing our own take on things.

**BB:** *What about the other projects you've got lined up?*

**MO:**  I guess the next thing that's popping out is one of the first things that I'm actually fully writing myself, that I'm not drawing at all, other than the cover. Image just picked it up. It'll be out in March 2003, and it's called *The Parliament of Justice*. It's drawn by Neil Vokes, and Neil kind of, I don't want to say "he's reinvented his style," because he's done this style before, but not in print. He's doing like an ink wash thing, and it looks just amazing. I was really shocked when I saw the first couple pages, because I got Neil to agree to draw it and I was just expecting the usual, dependable, nice work that Neil does. This great sense of energy stuff. And he started sending me these pages and they just blew me away. And Neil's been getting amazing reactions from other creators who've seen the work.

We actually got interest from DC. We were at a convention and one of their editors was like, "You should bring this up to WildStorm and Vertigo, and pitch it over there, because I really, really like this." But we decided not to, simply because Image gives us so much creative freedom that you just can't get at other companies, so we decided to just keep it there and not really show them. The whole issue's finished. It's a one shot, fifty-six pages.

It's not lettered yet. I still have to write the second draft of the script, because for me the dialogue is the most difficult thing. Especially when the art's already drawn, like in the old Marvel style [of working]. Because I supplied Neil with a script that was basically a page-by-page outline. You know, this is what happens on each page, blah-blah-blah. Actually, it was panel to panel, but Neil had the freedom to change whatever he wanted, but it was dialogue free. And in the end, we liked so much what he did that I really struggled with it, because I didn't want to cover up the art. So we kind of figured out a way to do it almost like a silent story, because it has definitely this sort of German Expressionist silent film feel to it. It's very stark, and contrasting, and abstract. So we found a way to work with it, and I'm really excited and I think people are really going to like it when it comes out.

**BB:** *I've seen about half of it, and what was there was pure dynamite. Absolutely some of the best stuff Neil's ever done, and that is saying a lot.*

**MO:** Yeah, Neil absolutely blew me away. Yeah.

And we've got some pinups in there. The main one, I guess, would be from Adam Hughes. He's going to do a piece for us, because Adam's both a friend of Neil's and a friend of mine. And we've got some other pieces in there from some friends, including a sketchbook section from myself, for the initial character designs and stuff.

But it's really Neil's show. I think people will like the story, but I really think that when people see Neil's work, they're just going to go crazy over it. It's definitely an adult book. The book won't have a mature readers label because I don't believe in those for comics, but all the advertisements and promotions and stuff will definitely let retailers and buyers know this is not a comic for kids.

**BB:** *It's for mature minds, in other words.*

**MO:** Yeah. Yeah, really mature minds. [*general laughter*] It's kind of like if the *Batman* 1960s TV show halfway through was replaced by a David Lynch version of the show. Or if David Fincher got his hands on it, you know? [*laughter*] It gets pretty strange.

**BB:** *Anything else coming up that's new which you can talk about now?*

**MO:** There are definitely other things, but at this point I'm talking about things that are so long-term that they wouldn't see fruition for another three years or so.

I guess the other thing I will mention is that, after the next *Hammer of the Gods* mini, there comes *Nevermore* from myself and Chris Golden, and then I have plans on doing a large, six-issue martial arts story that I plan on doing myself. And I'm real excited about that.

**BB:** *Is that a continuation of* Bastard Samurai *of sorts?*

**MO:** No, a whole other thing. So I look forward to starting that, because I studied some martial arts. That's one of my favorite hobbies. But I can't imagine I'll even start drawing that until probably this time next year.

**BB:** *Do you have a working title on that project?*

**MO:** Yeah, but I don't want to use that now. It's not that it's that special, but I'd just rather people not be asking me constantly about it between now and then, especially if something comes up to hold it up. Because often what happens is, if people know you're working on something, they'll ask you about it every time they see you. [*laughter*] And sometimes it'll put a false sense of focus on it. Especially because I have *Parliament* coming out, and *Nevermore* and *Hammer of the Gods*, so I want to make sure people are focusing on that.

**BB:** *Are you involved in any significant way with either the* Bulletproof Monk *or* Powers *films?*

**MO:** *Bulletproof Monk,* I was work for hire on. Which was good at the time, I mean I really needed the work, but it was also a valuable lesson to not do work for hire. Which is why I almost never do work for Marvel or DC, because I've gotten really, really attached to owning my own work. Especially if it's something that I'm creating, even if it's just a single character or something, I've just become so married to the idea of owning my own work that I don't even like to think about working for other companies because of that. Although I love those companies, and I definitely want to work with Marvel and DC in the future. But right now in my career, I just want to focus on my own stuff.

And working on *Bulletproof Monk* was a great experience because, it got me paying work, which I hadn't had in a long time. At the time it was a really low time in my career. And it was a great working experience, and it's great to be attached to the film. I'm only attached to it in name, as far as being able to promote myself and stuff, but that's cool. So I don't really have too much control over that. If I'm lucky, I'll get to pay $7.50 to see it. [*Laughter*]

**BB:** *So your design work and such aren't really being used in the production?*

**MO:** No. As far as I understand, and I saw the trailer of the film, I think the only thing it's really based on is the title, and just loosely on the concept of the book. I'm pretty sure they're kind of taking it in their own direction. Which is totally cool. That's what happens when you option a project. You know, it's about a zebra, and the first thing they want to get rid of is its stripes. [*general laughter*] But what I saw in the trailer looks really cool, and I'm excited to see it.

With *Powers*, it's just the opposite. Luckily, Frank Oz, who is now most interested in doing the film, and most likely is doing the film, actually wants some feedback from me, which is very cool. And him and Brian [Bendis] have had extensive phone conversations, and he's told him that, once he's ready to tackle the visual end of the film, he wants to get in touch with me and get some ideas of what I was thinking about in the book. He's definitely got a vision for the film, so I'm excited about it.

**BB:** *That's excellent. Any idea of when that might get a green light for actual production to begin?*

**MO:** Well, Frank's never had anything not green lit.

**BB:** *Hey, that's a good sign!*

**MO:** Absolutely. And Frank's a really good storyteller. He knows how to trim things from a story, how to sacrifice things from the story for the betterment [of a film]. I'm really, really excited about seeing his version of the film. Plus, he did a great thing by bringing Deena back into the script, because at one point Deena was taken out of the script. So he's definitely on the same page as Brian and I, and he has been having nice long conversations with Brian about it. So we're all real excited, you know?

**BB:** *Well, why don't we come back to the topic of* Powers *in a bit, and talk instead about how you got into comics and the road that got you to where you are today?*

**MO:**  Well, I guess it started when I was like twelve or so. We had moved down to Texas. I had lived in New Jersey all my life, and I really didn't like the move to Texas. [*Laughter*] Have you ever moved from one place to another when you were young?

**BB:**  *No. I had a fairly stable childhood as far as that's concerned.*

**MO:**  Ah. Yeah, it's pretty traumatic for a kid. Especially something so dramatic as going from New Jersey to Texas. Because, literally, it was like a whole other freakin' world, man. I could not adjust. I didn't like the heat. I didn't like the fact that there were no trees. I grew up in Jersey—people think of it as North Jersey—but most of Jersey is not like North Jersey; it's not factories and crap like that. It's mostly farm-land. A lot of trees, a lot of nature and stuff.

When we moved out to Texas, there was no nature yet. It was basically a desert where they had laid down carpets of grass. You know, rolled it out, temporary grass and trees that were no taller than me. And I'm short to begin with, so it was just deso-late. [*general laughter*] It was like living on a really cheap movie set, where they couldn't afford real trees or anything.

I would walk to the one store that was nearby, the 7-Eleven, and the ground was so dry there were cracks, huge cracks, in the ground. You know, like you see in dried mud, but they were like three feet wide and six feet deep. You could fall down these cracks, that's how dry the land was. And there weren't any lakes around, or anything. There was just nothing. Just completely barren.

So I didn't have much to do. I just locked myself into my room. I remember one of the most exciting things that could happen was Saturday mornings I would wait for that really bad D and D cartoon to show up. You know the one they made like six episodes of? And like every weekend I would just stay up all night to catch it in the early morning. And I was just so [annoyed], because every time it was a repeat. [*laughter*] I didn't know at that age they only made like six episodes, so I kept watching, waiting for new ones. I mean, that was my life, so it was pretty horrible. [*general laughter*]

I went with my mom to a flea market kind of thing, and I saw some comic books there. There was *Amazing Spider-Man*, and I forget the actual issue, but it was a Rich Buckler issue that had to do with some kind of vigilante who wore some kind of purple hood over his face or something stupid like that. And I absolutely loved it. And I remembered liking Spider-Man from the [Ralph] Bakshi cartoon show from the '60s, that was just so great and creepy. I would love watching that before going to school. And, for some reason, I have clear memories of reading *Spider-Man*, just a single issue of *Spider-Man*, in a barbershop. And I remember thinking, "Wow! Yeah, I like cartoons," and I remember *The Electric Company* with Spider-Man. So I dug them up, and I bought as many as I could, and I brought them home.

I had always kind of drawn a little bit, and my mom had always drawn, and I had an interest in drawing. But I had never really thought about comics until that point. I took them home, and I had myself some tracing paper, and just started tracing the images that I saw. I just traced for like a year, just constantly tracing and tracing. You know, tracing figures and then putting my own costumes on them, and kind of creating my own characters and then sending them into Marvel, saying, "Here, you can use this guy if you want," having no idea about copyright or anything like that. [*general laughter*] I just did that for a long time, until I finally started to try to draw for myself.

I started drawing, and I found a comic book store nearby. Then I met Adam Hughes, who was living in the town right over next to me. And we became friends, and Adam was one of my earliest mentors. He introduced me to Neil Vokes. Neil introduced me to a lot of my favorite artists now, like Mike Mignola's work, and Alex Toth, and Jack Kirby, and I learned a lot of storytelling from those people as well as from watching Adam work and grow.

When I met Adam, he wasn't doing *Justice League* or even *Maze Agency* or anything like that; he was getting rejected for *Jonny Quest* tryouts and stuff like that. I have some of his real early work. He had tried out for this book called *Justice Machine*, I think it was for some company in Texas, and I have his tryout pages from there from when he was in his John Byrne-out phase. So it was very funny to watch him grow from being rejected by companies to one of the best artists ever in comics. And, of course, we were real good friends, too. I learned a whole lot from him, just watching him and talking about comics and stuff.

So that's pretty much how it started out.

**BB:** *What did you learn from Adam?*

**MO:** A lot. I think, mostly, about storytelling. I really should have been just trying to rip him off and draw like him, I would have gotten work sooner if I had been one of those Adam clones. [*general laughter*] But luckily I had some sort of sense of self, and I found other people to rip off. [*more laughter*] But really, from Adam, it was talking about storytelling. And I remember specifically when he was working on the *Star Trek* graphic novel, and there's a scene of a bunch of guys getting out of a transport ship of some kind, like army guys, running. And he specifically pointed out to me how he had drawn each of them in like an animation phase. Like the first guy was like stepping out, the second guy was in a squatting, landing position, the third guy was running with his left foot out first, the next guy had his feet in the middle, and the next guy had his right foot out first, so it was like an animanics scheme. And we would talk about guys like Steve Rude, and why they were great. And it was really like a school in itself, talking about why we liked other artists and stuff, and Adam showing me what he was doing.

And one of the things I learned most from Adam was the thought process, which, for Adam, is—maybe it's changed, because we haven't worked together in a long time in the same studio—but at the time, when I was with him, he would take the longest on working on a page on looking at it. He would just stare at the page. It would be like freakin' blank, with like a couple lines, after an hour. He would just really, really think about the page and what he was doing before he started it. And that became a big thing for me, eventually, learning to really think about it. Even to this day, the thing that takes the longest for me is the breakdown stage, the layouts, and getting that right. Then the actual drawing, I just kind of [spit] it out, and there it is.

**BB:** *Well, how do you create a page these days?*

**MO:** Well, obviously, it starts with a script. On a page of *Powers*, it'll start . . .

If it's a panel of a six-panel grid, like if there's nothing going on, if it's just the heads talking, I prefer to do a grid. Because I really like the simplicity in that. If it's more complex, I'll do a little, tiny sketch, on the script, of how the panels will lay out. And then I'll either use eleven-by-seventeen photocopy paper, or regular legal-size paper, and I'll start doing sketches on that. That's where I do my breakdowns. And then I'll either blow it up, or I'll just transfer it directly using a light box. And that's where I spend all my time. I draw it in pencil, and then I take like a ballpoint pen and draw really tightly on top of that. So it's almost a finished drawing without the refined parts of it. In fact, usually when I go to conventions now, I bring my breakdowns with me and I'll sell them for like a buck or two, so everybody can walk away with something, because they're that close to being finished.

And then I do the light-box stage and, since it's already drawn so tightly, I can pretty much just go in straight with the pen and just start inking. In fact, right now, while I'm talking to you, that's what I'm doing. I'm just tracing some of my own drawings.

I never stopped tracing. [*general laughter*] I'm just a tracer.

**BB:** *What are some of you major concerns while you're doing that mentally intensive stage of discovering the layouts on the page?*

**MO:** Well, it depends what I'm working on. When I'm working on *Powers*—I'll take two different, polar-opposite books, *Powers* and *Hammer of the Gods*—when I get a page of *Powers*, it's very thought-intensive. Everything is done on purpose. Nothing's really done by accident, unless I'm just rushing through and really just trying to meet the deadline. Then it's more instinctual and that's when things can get a little bit sloppy and usually Pete Pantazis, our colorist, will have to fix something for me. But, generally, I'm very thought-intensive on it. I have to really pay attention to the script.

The first thing I have to figure out is how much is being said on the page. Because Brian is known for his dialogue and, obviously, some of the pages are very dialogue thick. Which is why, a lot of time in *Powers*, you'll see a lot of really thick gutters in between the panels. It's because I'm trying to make enough room. Instead of trying to make enough room on the panel for Ken Bruzenak, the letterer, to squeeze the lettering in, I'm leaving in blank space with the large tiers, so Ken will have plenty of room to lay it down. So that's one of the first things I'm thinking about on that page.

Then I'm thinking about, "Is this a day scene? Is it a night scene? Is it a light scene? Is it a dark scene?" because *Powers* is basically a noir book. But you can't have every page lit with noir lighting, because it will make the noir stuff less effective, it'll make the pacing less effective. So I have to figure out what is the tone of the page, and then I have fun with the tone. That will also dictate whether I'm using straight pen, or brush, or pen and brush. So there's just a lot of thought that has to go into a *Powers* page. And while *Powers* is like my home in comics, it's definitely work. I definitely have to think about what I'm doing.

Whereas *Hammer of the Gods* is more like a daydream on the page. Basically, I send Mark [Wheatley] like a really vague outline of the story, and then he'll send me back a step outline of the actual issue. And then I'll tighten up that step outline a little bit, and send it back to him. He'll send me back a script with, not panel [descriptions], but most of the dialogue on it, most of what's said. It's kind of the old Marvel style thing.

So then I can just go ahead [and draw it], and then it's like a daydream. And when I do a *Hammer of the Gods* page, I almost don't think at all. The best pages come out when I'm almost in a trance-like state. Like a painter, or a musician, [caught up in the flow of the moment]. You just kind of get into such a groove where the outside world kind of disappears, and I'm not thinking about time, or music, or anything.

And that becomes completely instinctual. I don't know what I'm doing on those pages until it's done. On that, there's almost no thought put into it, it's all like a daydream.

And I need that balance between *Powers* and *Hammer*. I need the thought-intensive, purposeful work with the daydream-like qualities of *Hammer*. If I was only doing *Hammer*, I would get bored with that and then I would need to create a project for myself that was more like *Powers*. And I need something like *Hammer* to offset *Powers*, because otherwise I could burn out. And my plan on *Powers* is to do it as long as Brian can hold up.

So they're two completely different approaches to storytelling.

**BB:** *Well, what strikes me about the approach to creating* Hammer *is the fact that that method might be one of the reasons you've been able to visually capture the ethereal, mythic quality so necessary to make that series work.*

**MO:** Thanks, man. Thanks.

**BB:** *That approach, relying on instinct, also seems like it's similar to the way Kirby is said to have worked. Just literally working at the page and discovering the story within that boundary. Except he was able to do it at* *that incredible pace—with no insult intended to you, of course!*

**MO:** [*laughter*] No. He made me look like Dave Stevens. The dude was incredibly fast. Just legendary. I guess we're doing the same thing—not talent-wise. I mean I can't compare to the originality of Kirby. Kirby was so original in what he did it's just mind-shattering. He was like the Jimi Hendrix of comics. But to an extent, it is playing for me, on *Hammer*. And I just kind of tap into the things . . .

Before I did *Hammer*, I studied a lot of Joseph Campbell's work. And I think that's really important, because if you can find the kind of universal things that click with people or what they can relate to, people who have no interest in Norse mythology, or are even repulsed by its Aryan roots, can dig it because, hopefully, it touches on different levels of what we're about as far as questioning God and your creator, and feeling out of place in the world.

So, hopefully, that daydreaming quality that I'm bringing to it when I'm drawing it, hopefully that comes across for people when they're reading it.

**BB:** *What kinds of tools are you using to create your pages these days?*

**MO:** [*laughter*] Pretty pitiful tools, man, since issue #16 or #17 of *Powers*. Early on, it was almost all brush.

Then it was a combination of brush and this pen called a Pigma Micron, which is kind of like a felt-tip pen. It's very respected by artists. A lot of artists use it. It's definitely a traditional tool. But then I was at like a Mailbox, Etc., and I was just standing in line, trying out some of their pens. And these ballpoint pens were just freaking amazing! It's a Uniball, it's called. And they don't fade, they're waterproof.

**BB:** *I know those pens; they're great writing instruments.*

**MO:** Yeah a lot of people just use Uniballs for just regular paperwork and stuff. So I got these two different sizes, and since like issue #16, I've started using them on *Powers*, and everything else I do. Pretty much all of *Powers*, like especially #18, where it's got [pretty much a] single line weight almost through the whole thing, that was all done with a Uniball, just a regular pen. And I pretty much abandoned most traditional tools. I still use a brush, and I've started finding a good balance between the two. Because I didn't like abandoning the brush completely, so I've been trying to find a good balance between the two.

As far as paper goes, I stopped using Bristol board and I don't use blue lined paper. I actually just go to Staples and I buy Hammermill. I use 54-pound cover stock, which is used for inkjet and laser printers, and it's just really thin and it comes in 11-by-17, so it's already the perfect size. It's very thin, and it's easy for me to see through, because I use the light box, so that was one of the important things for me. And, actually, some of the early *Hammer of the Gods* stuff, I actually did on photocopy paper, like straight photocopy paper. And that was just to try something different.

I like to break up the size I work at. Sometimes I draw *Powers* like 9-by-13.5, sometimes it's on a larger size. I just like breaking it up with different feelings and stuff. It keeps it from getting monotonous for me. Especially because, sometimes, my page rate goes really fast, depending what's going on on some of the pages. Like *Hammer of the Gods*, I can do probably four to five pages of pencils and inks in a day. On *Powers*, I typically do three pages of pencils and inks a day. So working on different formats and stuff helps me from, I don't want to say getting bored with the work, but getting bored with the process.

**BB:** *Do you vary the size according to the nature of the particular story being told? Because I can imagine, if you've got all this dialogue that has to be put down, especially when you've got a lot of those talking head shots, you might want to do that larger.*

**MO:** Well, sometimes it's easier to do it smaller, too. Like when I have a double page spread, I almost always turn the page sideways and do the page that way, instead of actually doing it on two pieces of paper, even if it has a lot of dialogue, because it's being done in computer, and Ken's a very talented letterer, he can adjust to whatever size that I use. It doesn't really play into that much of a factor. And, actually, those pages where Brian's got a lot of people talking, a lot of other artist's say, "Oh, God, I could never do that," or, "That looks so difficult," it's really not. Those are really the easiest pages. I've had pages where it's all talking heads, and I can do like eight pages in a day, pencils and inks, because you're just drawing heads. You're drawing heads, and some backgrounds, and people talking. What gets difficult is when I have to draw buildings, because I want the buildings to look like a New York City, Chicago, Detroit. You know, a really nice-looking city. When there's cars—god forbid I have to draw a dog! That takes a lot of time. That stuff's tough for me to draw.

But you give me some talking heads pages, and I could do a book in three days. Talking heads are easy, so I always welcome a talking heads page. And a double-page splash, because I draw a double-page splash on one page. So when I do a double-page splash, I get it done in the time it takes to do one page. So it's like, "Woo-hoo! I just did two pages in three hours!" or something. [*general laughter*]

**BB:** *Are we talking about an eight-hour day, a twelve-hour work day typically?*

**MO:** It ranges. I had a bunch of crap to do earlier. I got up about 9 o'clock. I originally [was] just going to go out and do a bunch of photocopies, come back and work at home. But then, because I have a family and they're at home, and I work at home, those plans shift pretty quick. I started work at about 12, and I did three pages of pencils and inks this morning, between now and then, which is almost 3 o'clock. Now granted, one of the pages is like a big, blank page with a TV screen in the middle of it, but I still count it as a page, though. [*laughter*] So, hopefully, today, I'll probably work until about 4:30, and then I've got some family stuff to do. So a day of work can range from four hours to eight or nine hours. And some days I don't get any work done. Because I work at home, it's all a great blessing and a curse, you know?

**BB:** *Do family concerns break up the day?*

**MO:** It breaks up the day a lot, and it's a big concern for me, because I have a wife and a child. If I didn't have a family, I would probably be working constantly. I'd be one of those guys . . .

I think everybody knows the artist who lives in an efficiency apartment, and spends all of his money on Sega games, or PlayStation or whatever. Pizza boxes all over the place, and they never shower, and all they do is work. That is what I'd be if I didn't have a family. So the family keeps me sane.

It's a big problem for me to balance family time and work time, because I do love working so much. But, obviously, I want to spend time with the family as well. Like right now, one of the reasons I'm trying to do so much work is because people care about my work. So I'm trying to take advantage of that because, five years from now, people might not care. We know a lot of really good, talented artists who, for absolutely no reason, people just aren't interested in seeing their work anymore. And I'm prepared for that to happen, because it happens. And what I'm hoping is that I can create enough of a body of work so that, when *Powers* is done, which hopefully won't be for a very long time, when *Powers* is finished, people will remember a lot of the work that I did on my own and be excited to see more stuff from me. So that's what I'm doing now.

Pretty much, the plans that I have now take me into the next two and a half years. Once those two and a half years are done, I plan on cutting every-thing out except for *Powers* and *Hammer of the Gods*. That way I'll have a lot more time to spend with family, and get to have more of a life and get to do the things normal people do. [*laughter*] My son is in first grade now, he'll be starting that next week, and once he starts, I plan on getting up really early in the morning. [So I'll be] getting up at quarter to five in the morning, and putting in about three hours of work, getting him up, and taking him to school, coming back home, and then work from 9 to like 3 o'clock, when I'll pick him up, and then spend the day with family, and then go to bed early. And that way I can get a good amount of work [done] and see the family at the same time. It's definitely a struggle, and it's definitely an issue in the household, not getting to spend enough time with the family.

***BB:*** *Are you able to take time off on the weekends, or do you have to work some of them, too?*

**MO:** Some of the weekends I work through, too.

***BB:*** *And that has got to hurt things a bit. Because it seems that it really helps if you're able to take at least one or two days a week just to be with them.*

**MO:** Yeah, definitely. Usually, I try to take at least one day of the weekend off. Ninety percent of the time I can. And even when I do have to work through two days of the weekend, because I work at home, I can take a Wednesday off, or I'm just sure to have dinner with everybody at night, and go to the movies, or something. And I still think that I end up spending more time [with them] than say the average working family, even on my worst days. Because they can see me at any point, and I can see them at any point, but it's still not the same thing as quality time.

**BB:** *What kind of pencils, ink, and brushes are you using today, and how do those compare with the tools you used to use?*

**MO:** I started out, like a lot of people, using technical pens. Rapidiographs, I used to ink with those, because I was told that's what inkers use. Same thing with the pencil. I used to use a mechanical pencil, where you put the lead inside and it's got that cool grip thing on the front, it's like a draftsman pen. And this is all stuff [I used] because I thought it made me feel more like an artist, or more like a professional. And it took me a long time to realize that it's how you're using it, not what you're using.

So, even with pencils now, I guess I use a professional pencil, I can only get it at an art store. It's called a ProArt Graphite Drawing. I use a 3H. And sometimes I'll just use the regular 2H with an eraser on it, like you use for school. And ink, I'll pretty much use anything. I'm pretty cheap with that stuff, I really don't care. I know a lot of artists and a lot of inkers, like Karl Story or Brian Stelfreeze, they only use a specific brand of ink. I think Brian Stelfreeze actually mixes his own inks.


**BB:** *I'd believe it.*

**MO:**  Yeah. He's got this whole set up where he hangs his brushes up in a certain way so that when they dry a certain way. My place is a freakin' mess. It looks like somebody shook the house in my studio. Pens are all over the place. Piles of paperwork. It's very anarchic. [*laughter*] Pens that haven't worked in three or four years are up here, next to my desk.

So I usually use Higgins Black Magic ink, just because that's what my local art store carries, and then I'll water it down, to make it last longer. It's not like I can't afford to buy new ink, it's just that I don't want to have to go out and get some. And then what's strange is it starts to stink after a while. Like the ink really gets this weird smell from mixing water in it. I think maybe it's getting mold inside the ink or something. I'm not sure. Maybe I shouldn't be inhaling it, I don't know. [*general laughter*]


**BB:** *So it sounds like you're not that worried about having perfectly opaque blacks.*

**MO:** No, not at all. Not at all.

One of my favorite artists, Mike Mignola, I've got a bunch of his work. And I just love looking at the brush strokes on his original pages. I can see exactly where he laid it down heavier and lighter, because he uses a really thin ink. I don't know why, but that's what he does.

I really admire Karl Story, or Brian Stelfreeze, or Jason Martins. They look like printouts. When you look at their pages, they're so perfect they're like printouts, and I love that. But I can't do that with my own work. It's time consuming.

I'm all about speed. Get that stuff done. Adam said about me that I learned how to draw fast, and then I learned how to draw good, which I think is true.

**BB:** *Did you start hitting your stride when you began to focus on how the whole page was designed, and combining that with your panel-to-panel storytelling concerns?*

**MO:** Well, that comes from my influence from Brian Bendis. Before I worked on *Powers* . . .

There's really only two works of mine that you can look at before *Powers* that shows my kind of progression: one was *Ship of Fools*, which is almost completely lacking and devoid of design. It's all just panel-to-panel stuff. In fact, it's just way too crowded, and it's very hard to breathe and to follow, and it's just panel-to-panel work. It was before my style changed, where my work became iconic and easier to look at, so I was trying to do a lot of line work and stuff. So it was just a lot harder to look at.

Then, after that, my very next work was *Bulletproof Monk*. And *Bulletproof Monk* was the first time I really paid attention to the design. I'd bought a bunch of design books, and I had become friends with David Mack over the years, and I really liked the way he would use design, and put his sense of design into the pages. So I took a combination of that, and I had just met Brian Bendis at the beginning of *Ship of Fools*, and we became friends during *Ship of Fools*, and started paying attention to his design work. So it was a combination of learning from those two, and importing design into *Bulletproof Monk*. Which just came out in trade. And, even though it's three years old, and it's before my style kind of changed, I'm still very happy with it. So that was the first time I started paying attention to design.

Then, once *Powers* started, that's when I really started taking cues from Brian and learning a lot about designing a clearer sense of storytelling. Partially from his panel layouts, and partially from the transition of styles that I was going through, when I was picking up more on the Bruce Timm and Alex Toth stuff. That was a huge, huge help.

**BB:** *What aspects did you pull from Toth?*

**MO:** It took me a long time to learn from Toth, he's so deceptive. It's so difficult to look at his work and figure out exactly what he's doing. So, early on, I think I'd first become aware of his work when I was doing *Footsoldiers*. And if you look at *Footsoldiers*, there's a lot of black there, but I don't think I understood how I was using it. It just took me a lot of years to decipher what it was about Toth that I loved, and what was so strong about his work. And I don't think it really clicked until I hit my Bruce Timm interest, and then, with a combination of the two, like somehow learning more about Bruce's work opened up my eyes to what it was about Toth's work that worked, and vice versa. Then, once I'd gotten to there, and I figured out simplifying the form, taking out the lines and stuff, and combining that with the use of black in composition, that's when things clicked in together.

I think largely from Toth, it was just simplifying. Which, oddly enough, it takes years to learn how to simplify. I was reading . . . I forget where the quote comes from; it might be from Robert McKee's book on story. It was a quote about somebody who had written somebody else a letter, it was a lengthy letter, and then ended it by apologizing, saying that they wished they had more time to write a shorter letter—because it takes more time to learn how to simplify things. And that's absolutely true. It took me years to learn how to get simple, and that's largely what I learned from Toth.

**BB:** *That's a really interesting and telling observation, because, in the common wisdom, it should be easier. After all, you have to draw fewer lines if it's simple, right? But that's simply not true, is it? Those lines left are so important.*

**MO:**  Oh yeah. Well, especially when you grow up like I did, loving somebody like Art Adams. [*general laughter*] Art Adams, and Michael Golden, these guys to me were gods! Or Moebius, all that little line work stuff. I just absolutely loved it. I spent so much time trying to be Art Adams when I was younger, and then, later on, trying to be Michael Golden or Kevin Nowlan, and just not learning to be myself. And it was only when I learned to be myself that I was able to take the influences that I had, like Toth and Bruce Timm, and open it up into whatever it was the way I saw it.

So it's really, really, really difficult to do just simple lines. Sometimes even now, I struggle. I want to get it simpler. I look at guys like Paul Grist on *Kane*, it's like, "God, if I could only do that!" If I could get that simple, that would be great.

I don't fill in the blacks on my art. Pretty much, on my original pages, I just put an "x" there and then

I'll let the letterer or the colorist or whoever fill in the blacks for me, because it just saves time. And sometimes I'll do that on my own, where I'll fill in the black on computer, and I'll accidentally hit the wrong spot, and it'll blacken a whole other area that I hadn't thought of and it looks ten times better. But it covers up a drawing I like, so I'll be the sucker. I'll take the easy way out, which is to keep what I originally had because I liked the drawing. When, if I was being more pure to the artwork, if I was being more truthful to what the art should be saying, that I would go that route where I black out the things that I liked that I drew, and made it more simple.

When Mignola draws a page, he draws everything. I've seen his pencils, and the dude, he draws everything. He's very detailed. And then he's able to go through and sacrifice everything to the brush and just black it all out. He's amazing.

**BB:** *It's also fairly time consuming, to draw all of that detail and then just cover it all.*

**MO:** It does. I timed myself on a page of *Powers*. It took me twenty minutes to fill in a black. Which doesn't sound like a lot, but if I'm doing three pages a day, that twenty minutes adds up to almost another hour of work. I could get another page done, or almost get another page done.

**BB:** *Why don't you take us through the process, step by step, of making a page? Say you've just gotten the latest* Powers *script from Brian, or that step plot from Mark for* Hammer. *Do you read the whole script first, before you put pen to paper, or do you start in right away?*

**MO:** I pretty much have to read the whole thing through. When I was doing the *Bluntman and Chronic* book, I was having a lot of trouble because that's when my schedules were conflicting. Because the schedules weren't exactly how they started out to be, so things really started conflicting and I had a lot of problems keeping up with deadlines. And for a couple issues, I wasn't reading the issues all the way through. As I was drawing, I would read each page as I did it. And that was a real detriment because you really need to know what's going on in the rest of the issue, because of such things as foreshadowing. You also have to know sometimes details are left out of the script, which you won't find until after you've done other pages later.

So, pretty much as a rule, unless I'm absolutely, 100 percent desperate, which hasn't happened in a while, I have to read the script all the way through. And I suggest that to everybody. I suggest that for the letterer and the colorist, as well. Everybody really should know what's going on in the story as you tackle it.

So I'll read the whole script through. I'll look at the page; if it's a page that's particularly crammed with stuff, I'll put a little star next to the panel that has to be the largest or draw the most attention. Then I'll do the little tiny thumbnail breakdown of the panels. And then I'll actually start to break that down on a page. That takes the longest, drawing it the first time, because that's when I have to make sure the eyes are level, and stuff like that. That's when all the real work comes in. And actually drawing and inking the page is easy and fun.

**BB:** *And probably goes the quickest, too.*

**MO:** Absolutely. It's really fast. The thing that takes the longest is drawing the breakdowns.

**BB:** *Now, when you're first starting out, going from those thumbnails through the next few steps in the penciling process, do you vary the thickness of your lead's tip?*

**MO:** Right now, for the last couple of months—like I said, for a while, I was drawing everything with a monotone line weight—but recently what I started doing is, I'll draw everything with a monotone line weight, then I'll go in afterwards, with a brush, and start putting variations with a brush. Because I like both. So sometimes it'll be bare line weights, and then other times it'll be a combination of monotone line weight with a brush. I like both, but I'm still feeling things out and trying different things.

**BB:** *What are some of the things that you've learned from Brian?*

**MO:** For me, the main thing I got from Brian was pacing; learning how to slow down, how to really take your time telling a story. And that's a tricky thing to say, especially for people starting out, because the danger is you won't have the time to take to tell your story, because your book will get freakin' canceled before you have the time to get to the set part. But at the same time, if you just go ahead and start with conflict, before there's any sense of what's at risk, then it doesn't work. And if you look at *Powers*, and you look at the really slow growth between Walker and Deena, between their characters, there's some crap that's coming up there that people are absolutely going to love; and they're going to love it ten times better because it's happening in issue #25, instead of happening in issue #4. And it makes the characters that much more real to people. So, in both the sense of writing . . . I think, actually, most of my writing style that I have now, I've picked up from working with Brian. It just comes from working with him, you know? So definitely my writing, and my visual pacing, has been very influenced by Brian's work. Which, in turn, has been very influenced by guys like Howard Chaykin, and his set of influences, and how he interpreted those influences, as well.

And then, of course, Chaykin was influenced by Toth, who was influenced by Hugo Pratt, who was influenced by blah-blah-blah and it just keeps on going. Which is why if you ever send a letter to Alex Toth, the thing he just drills into your head is, "Just draw from life," and there are so many people to learn from, other than the comic book people.

**BB:** *Do you prefer a full script, or that Marvel-style plot outline?*

**MO:** It depends on what I'm working on. Obviously on *Powers*, I prefer the full script. But it's also because Brian and I have become so simpatico with our work, we're so much, literally, on the same page, that as soon as he says something I see it in my head, as soon as it's in the script, I see it in my head. We've got like a secret language of some sort, where all he kind of has to do is say, "Do this to that," "Change this thingie into that thingie," or, "The thingie doesn't work." "Thingie" is often a word we use in our conversations. [*laughter*] He'll say, "Change the thingie, I don't like the thingie," and I'll know what he's talking about and will just go ahead and do it. We've become really close in our storytelling and stuff.

Obviously with *Hammer*, I like the looseness, the daydreaming quality of it.

I just recently worked with a script for DC for a short story, and it was a great script, a great writer, but it was so outside of the process that I'm used to working in, I didn't enjoy it as much. Not the work, but actually doing the work. I'm just absolutely spoiled on my own process and having my own freedoms and stuff.

So I don't really have an answer for you, which I prefer to work on. I think that's why, eventually, I want to break everything down to only working on *Powers* and working on *Hammer*, because they are polar opposite books. Which I think my fans will enjoy both; if you like what I'm drawing, I think, then, you'll like both books. But they're polar opposites as far as the way they're executed, and the way they're read, and everything.

**BB:** *Do you ever vary much from what Brian's described in the script?*

**MO:** Oh no. No. Sometimes I'll omit things, again, for the whole simplifying aspect. Rarely, I'll add something. I rarely, rarely ever change anything.

Most of the ways that I affect the script is I'll just give Brian some feedback. Like I'll say that, "This was great, but at the end Deena says something to Walker, and it takes me out of the moment. Maybe you shouldn't have her do that." You know, just really minor stuff like that. Basically just giving Brian some feedback. But I've never felt the need to change anything.

At the same time, Brian respects me enough that I have the freedom to do so if I want to. But, like I said, it's a super rare occasion. In fact, I can't think of anything major, after twenty-five issues.

**BB:** *Let's talk a little about the influences that Neil's had on you. What were some of the things that you learned from him?*

**MO:** He taught me a lot about loosening up with my work. Because I was very anal with the work, early on. I was in my Art Adams phase, and trying to keep everything perfect. And he really taught me how to loosen up on the page.

And I met Neil during the most interesting part of my career, I guess. [*laughter*] That was when I was working for this small company called Comics Zone, with my buddy, Rich Rankin. And we did lots of exploitation and porn books.

My very first printed work was with a company called Innovation, and it was a book called *Newstralia*. I had inked the story when I was like fourteen. I was still in high school. That was pretty exciting. But I was too stupid to know that I should just keep looking for more work after that, so I never even tried again after that gig, until years later when I started working for the same company again. I did *Child's Play*, and I did that for about a year and a half.

And that's when I met Neil and Rich, and they got me drawing porn at the age of eighteen. And when I was there, I had met my buddy Brian Glass, through a local role-playing game. And we started writing this thing and drawing it, at the time it was called *Micro Spandex* and it was kind of a '70s superhero parody thing. And Brian and I did that for a while, and that got me noticed and pulled me to DC where I started working way too early for the big guys. Pat Garrahy, who later on became the colorist of *Powers*, was working at Marvel and got me some gigs inking *Daredevil* during the "Fall from Grace" period. So that was really neat, working with Daredevil. He's such a neat character.

It was shortly after that that the *Micro Spandex* thing came out, and I started getting penciling work from DC, and one of them was *Judge Dredd*. And *Judge Dredd* was cool, but it was completely bad timing.

I wasn't ready to be drawing a book yet; I was just in the right place at the right time. I had just enough talent to make them think I was very good. [*general laughter*] And it was a very valuable learning lesson, and I definitely value those days—even though I think that it did hurt me being on that book. Not being on the book, but getting the work when I did, because I just wasn't ready for it yet. So people, I think especially at DC, really associated me with that work—which wasn't all that good. So it was a lesson learned in patience. But I definitely value those times, the friendships that I made with both the editors and writers, like Andy Helfer, at the time.

And then, from there, I did *Footsoldiers* by Jim Krueger. Jim and I have been friends ever since, and I formed a good relationship with Dark Horse because of it. Then after *Footsoldiers*, things started drying up, and there was a combination of stuff. Like inking Neil on *Ninjak* for a year, and starting *Ship of Fools*. And then, after that, it dried up. Then I went to *Bulletproof Monk*. And then my career completely dried up, and that's when I kind of I gave up on things and got a security job. [*laughter*]

**BB:** *You know, a lot of people would have just kissed the business good-bye forever at that point. This gets right back to the fact of how important your family is to you.*

**MO:** Yeah. Well, my wife, I've been with her since I got out of high school. And she's always been supportive—and mostly financially supportive. She paid the bills while I was trying to get my career going. And sometimes I was able to pay the bills, but for the most part, I wasn't. I wasn't able to pitch in my half, and I refused to get a real job because I felt that I had talent and I knew there was good money to be made; that if I got suckered into a regular job, I would be pulled away from a better life as an artist. So I never had any kind of fallback plan or anything. So it was always being a comic book artist. Like, I never had a real job until things dried up so badly that I got out of comics. And, at that point, I had no choice, because I had a son. So it was a big difference from before, where the wife could go away and work, we're living in an apartment, blah-blah-blah, to where you have a son and a house.

So that's when I got a regular job. It was definitely a good thing to get out of comics, and clear my head up. And that was a really valuable experience.

**BB:** *And you were gone for how long, about a year, two years?*

**MO:** Yeah, about a year I guess.

**BB:** *But you kept drawing the whole time, right? I mean you have to do something to stay awake when you're* *a security guard, especially if you happened to be on the night shift.*

**MO:**  Yeah. Well, that's why I got the job. Even giving up, I was still so stubborn that I got myself a job where I could still draw. That was why I got the security job. But that's also how and why I had started simplifying my work, because I knew if I was going to do any other comics, that basically they would have to be four-issue miniseries, it would have to be a hit-and-run kind of thing, you know? Do the comics and then move on to whatever the next idea was. So, because of the limited time that I had to draw, because I was working the regular job and helping to raise a child . . .

I was being Mr. Mom. The wife was away working, making the real money, I was working on the weekends and raising our kid during the day. So everything he does now is my fault because I was exposed to him way too much early on. So I had to simplify my stuff a lot, and that's when I started to do *Hammer of the Gods*, when I was just learning to do a really simple style. And when you look at the first couple issues of *Hammer of the Gods*, you can see the progression of when I was still doing too much detail, to later on, when I was learning to loosen up and get rid of it.

But the most important thing that the job taught me was a sense of self-worth. That I could have a family, have a regular job, and still be an artist. I didn't need to be in the Wizard Top 10, or have a book that was making money, or have any kind of comic book success to still be an artist. Because I was still doing work. I was doing work and selling it on eBay. Doing watercolors, which I hadn't ever done before, and was very happy with. By getting a real job, and being forced into that situation, I got a sense of self-worth as an artist that I never had before. And a great sense of security, because I know, if things go south on me again, I can always go ahead and get another security job and still do my comics on the side and still be an artist.

The books I'm currently doing aren't what define me as a person. It's so much more than that now. It's very Zen, but sometimes you have to take four or five steps backwards to move forward at all.

**BB:** *In a real sense, it's a classic case of making lemonade after life had given you a lemon. And the result of all that is what is, it seems, a renaissance of sorts for you.*

**MO:** That's what it was, definitely. It absolutely was. It was a huge change for me. It was a huge blessing.

I really hated it at the time. That was the first real job I ever had. The only other jobs that I had, I'd washed dishes as a teenager and then, when I was able to get a driver's license, I delivered pizzas for a while, which was a lot of fun. But neither of those were real jobs. They were absolutely under the table, and free of responsibility. So that was the first time I'd ever had real work, and it's was real important to do that. And that's why I think I'm so appreciative of the success that's going on now, is because of that time period. Because I know it can all go away, and that, if it does, I'll be fine with it.

**BB:** *What were some of the other lessons you got early on from Neil?*

**MO:** Neil just really introduced me to a lot of artists I otherwise wouldn't have looked at. And I think one of the most important things I get from Neil, when you're actually talking about the page, is a sense of environment. When you look at Neil's pages, everything's on there. You look at a page and you really feel a world. You don't just see the characters in the foreground. He's just got so much going on in the backgrounds, and they feel so real and alive. He's got such a great sense of environment that often, when he's slow in work, I'll hire him to do backgrounds for me. Which he did a lot of, he did a lot of backgrounds and layouts and stuff, especially on *Bluntman and Chronic*. And he laid out issue #11 of *Powers* for me, because that was the same time I was on *Bluntman and Chronic*, and my deadlines were crashing in to each other. So that's why the backgrounds in there are so good. [*general laughter*] Otherwise, it's more close-ups of heads. [*more laughter*]

**BB:** *Who taught you how to approach the companies and editors, and how to pursue work?*

**MO:** Nobody, really. That actually came out of habit, from writing Mike Baron. When I was younger, one of the first books that I really fell in love with was *Nexus*. Just on a whim, I decided to write Mike Baron and show him some artwork, and he wrote back. And we just kept writing back and forth, and it just kind of set up in my mind that that was how it was done, "Well, let me start showing my work to some editors, just to get some feedback, just like Mike Baron." So that's what I started doing, and the feedback became rejections, and rejections became work offers—and then rejections again. [*general laughter*]

**BB:** *What were some of the things you learned from the whole Marvel-DC experience? It seems like, on the whole, it was a good experience for you.*

**MO:** Oh yeah. Even *Judge Dredd* was a good experience, even though, at the time, I didn't know it was a good experience. What I learned from *Judge Dredd* was how to talk to editors. I learned how to say "No." I saw myself as the wonder boy. I was like twenty, just turning twenty-one, and I was on the flagship title for this new line of *Judge Dredd* books, which was going to be huge. I should have started out first by putting my foot down about the schedule, because the schedule, if I remember correctly, it just didn't give me enough time. I think I was working on issue #3 or #2 when issue #1 came out. Also, I was penciling and inking it. I should have just penciled it. Actually, I should have just said, "No," that I wasn't ready at all, and I shouldn't have even freakin' tried. So, it was just a lot of lessons to be learned. [*laughter*]

I just was not ready, and then I burned out. And it was very unprofessional on my part, as far as I was just trying too hard for something that I just wasn't ready for yet. But also, nobody put limits on me, so I didn't know that I wasn't ready for it. So, with DC, it was just a lot of learning about how to conduct myself as a professional and deal with other people. I never threw any fits or tantrums or anything—that I know of, or was told of. But I did learn about how to just communicate better with the editors.

And meeting deadlines. I was always good at meeting deadlines, except for *Judge Dredd*, and except for *Powers*, when things got out of hand after I took on *Bluntman and Chronic*. That's an important thing for me: being on time, getting the work done.

I can't say there was too much to learn from working at Marvel and DC. I think largely it's because you're an art monkey over there. Marvel and DC, you really don't have any freedoms. You have to answer to editors. A lot of editors don't like you communicating with the other creators on books, which is absolutely backwards and bizarre to me. I don't think DC even, until recently, was using scanned artwork. You couldn't even send in your artwork digitally until recently. And they still do weird things, like I don't understand editors dictating stories versus the writers dictating stories. There's just a lot of artistic freedom that you're not exposed to over there. And then, once you get it, you'll never want to go back.

I'm not criticizing them or anything like that, I'm just saying that I've had this completely opposite exposure to that [than most creators]. I know huge, great famous artists are making tons of money and are doing great. But I still look at them like slaves. I still look at them, like, "What are you doing working for these dudes? They're making a lot of money! You're making a decent living, but these are your cre-ations, and your images, and your ideas, and you're selling yourself short." That's how I see working for Marvel and DC, unless you're working on *Batman*, or *Spider-Man*, or *Daredevil*—you know, something special. Otherwise, I just don't understand it anymore.

**BB:** *In other words, if you came up with, and this is off the top of my head, your version of "Born Again" or another real, solid* Daredevil *tale, you'd have no problem doing that, then?*

**MO:** If I came up with a great *Daredevil* story, the first thing I would ask myself is, "Do I need to do this with Daredevil? Is there a way I could take Daredevil out of it, and keep it for myself?" And if the answer's "Yes," then that's what I'll do. If the answer's "No," then maybe I'll talk to Marvel about it.

Marvel and DC are great to work for for exposure. They're great to work for because they're so respected. Image, I think, has started to gain a lot more respect over the years, but there's still nothing quite like working for the Godfathers of comics, Marvel and DC.

**BB:** *Or that Godfather and your wicked uncle, Marvel. [general laughter]*

**MO:** For a long time, I had no interest in working for Marvel. But they've started doing things that were so interesting, largely, just giving power back to the writers. I don't specifically mean just Bendis, because they were doing that before they hired Brian. They had started making some real interesting choices, and allowing the writers to decide the destiny of the characters. See, I think editors . . . I'm going to make myself some enemies here, but I don't think editors should be doing what they're doing. I think editors are putting their noses in sections where they just don't belong in. Editors should be there to keep a book together, to organize everything, to say, "This is what the tone of the series is." But not to say, "All right, we're going to have this big story about so-and-so." They're almost writing plots for the writers, and telling the writers what they should do. And, in some cases, even worse: telling writers they have to deal with these other writer's plots. I know great writers who are being shackled by freakin' editors who are giving them other crappy writers' story plots to deal with.

**BB:** *Seriously?*

**MO:** Oh yeah! I know guys who left DC because of it. Especially with the crossovers. How would you like being a writer, and there's another writer who, say you like as a friend, but you think that their stories are just stupid? And then you're told you have to pick up their story and go with it? That's crazy. And when an editor does that, they're insulting the writer. Not just in a way that's disrespectful, but they're doing it in a way that's shackling their talents and making them look bad.

Also, I don't see why editors are writing out word balloons. Ken Bruzenak is a letterer who's got . . . God, I don't know how long he's been in the business.

Almost twenty years? Do you think he needs an editor to put little circles on photocopies to tell him where to put the word balloons? Why are editors doing that? It's insane!

I think the editors should be more like producers, where they're kind of setting the tone, the general direction of the books, but really they just have to leave it up to the writers. And if they want to write, then stop being an editor and start writing.

**BB:** *Now, I don't think that you want to take away their power to make story suggestions or corrections if there's something that doesn't really work, or is just wrong, correct?*

**MO:** Not at all.

**BB:** *Right. Your problem is with the practice of dictating story specifics.*

**MO:** Yeah. Yeah, definitely. There's a difference between suggesting, or even dictating, the tone of the story. That's fine if you're dictating the tone of the book. I mean, if you're doing the X-Men and somebody is trying to turn it into Ambush Bug, well, then, obviously no matter how good the writer is, you're not going to let him or her do that. That's what an editor's for—to keep the boat steady. But I think too many times editors are in the way. They're just in the way. And writers need editors, and artists need editors, but they need them for feedback. In my opinion, they need them for feedback, to keep them grounded and keep them in the right direction, but not to write the stories for them.

Which is, a lot of times, that's what they're doing. Sometimes they create characters and tell the writer to put them in there. That's just weird.

I think that's why a lot of books are crap. [*general laughter*] Most of them are unreadable. I can't read most comics because they just don't make sense. You pick up an issue, pick up three issues, you pick up four issues, and you still don't know what's going on? Can you imagine trying to watch a TV show like that?

**BB:** *Yet it's not because of a slowed-down pacing, as you were discussing with* Powers.

**MO:** But I think, sometimes, that is a problem in some comics. Too much is happening at once. It's either that, or the first thing that turns me off about a book is exposition. And that's not a little exposition, but blatant exposition. Like people . . .

I talk to myself when I'm in a room, and there's nobody else around, but I don't have complete conversations that, if somebody else was listening to, they'd be able to figure out all my motivations for the day. And that's what happens. I'll read a book, and somebody's in a room by themselves, and they'll say out loud exactly what they're thinking. And nobody says exactly what they're thinking, especially when you're talking to yourself! You go, "Where's that book?" You never say, "Where's the book that has the evidence that so-and-so was with so-and-so that did blah-blah-blah-blah," like explaining a plot. I mean, that's what people are doing in comics, and that's just bad, bad, bad, bad, bad writing. And that's, I'd say, 70 percent of the comics. Ah, 90 percent of the comics. And it starts with exposition.

**BB:** *What are some of the other problems you see with a lot of comics these days?*

**MO:** Just no understanding of story. What to focus on.

*Ship of Fools* is a perfect example of that, and it's not Brian Glass's fault. Brian was dealing with my whimsies. [*laughter*] You know, I wanted to do weird stuff, and I would throw weird crap at him that had nothing to do with the plot or structure, and that he would have to fit it in there. And I was having a lot of fun, but we were telling a story that was impossible to follow, because of the same reasons.

So, one of the problems we had, that I think most people have with their book, is they don't know what it's about. Ask a person what their book is about, and a lot of times, they just don't know. They'll say, "It's about cool stuff," or, "It's about these guys who are like on this team, and they're outlaws," and it's a cliché! And everything they pull out is stuff you've heard before.

I know there are a lot of good comics out there, I just don't seem to find them. When I do find them, they're in trade paperback. Paul Pope's *Heavy Liquid*. I love Paul Pope's work. And when I first saw *Heavy Liquid*, I tried reading it and I just couldn't understand it, or I couldn't follow it. Also, just because of the way my life's structured, I was missing issues. And then I got the trade and I read the trade, and I was just like, "Oh my god, this is so great!" It was just one of the best things I've ever read. And what was great was he took a three-act story structure, he twisted it around a little bit so that it wasn't predictable—because with a regular three-act story structure you know when things are going to happen, just because of the structure, and he played around with it just enough, and it was just great.

And Brian Azzarello with *100 Bullets*. I love that writing, it's great stuff. And a lot of writing just has to do with personal taste. I'm not saying I'm right in my opinions; it's just my opinions.

**BB:** *Any other books that you think are particularly well written these days?*

**MO:** Well, of course, [Mike Mignola's] *Hellboy*. But *Hellboy* is good for the opposite reasons that things like *100 Bullets* or *Powers* or *Alias* [are good]. *Hellboy* is good because it doesn't follow a structure, and because it just kind of ... It doesn't make itself up as it goes along, it just doesn't really follow any rules. But it does it in such a way that it has its own rules, but they're kind of secret rules. Like, you don't really know why Mike's doing something, and he doesn't know why he's doing something, but it always works. And think that just comes from Mike having years of experience as a storyteller. I think that's the kind of thing you have to develop, it doesn't happen overnight.

There are a lot of other good books out there. Paul Dini's books are always good. Paul blows me away because he can write a complete story in twenty-two pages or less. That's completely brand-new, with characters you don't know who they are, and he just sets everything up and the exposition's there, in just the right amount of levels, and he's just a great writer. He's able to just do something with so little.

He's like the Alex Toth of writers. [*general laughter*] He's one of my favorite guys, too.

I know I sound a lot more negative in print than I am in real life, but I just wish to see better writing in comics. And I know there are other good books and stuff out there, I just don't get to read as often as I'd like to. I guess I'm a very "The glass is half empty" guy, so usually I just look around [at the comic racks] and go, "Oh, crap. Crap. Crap." [*laughter*]

There's a lot of good writing going on, but it's crippled by a lot of bad writing. And I think that the writing that's going on right now is ten times better than [before]. If you think that I think that comics are bad now, in the '90s they were unreadable. Just unreadable. And I'm not just saying that in the way that everybody looks back and then hacks up the last decade or something. I mean, really, the '90s were just full of crap. I mean just nothing to read. A generation of comic book writers growing up reading comic book writers and just learning how to write from just comic books.

In my own writing—I hope I'm not setting myself up for harsh criticism, because I'm just learn-ing to write myself. I've been studying, and I know how hard it is to write stories from trying to write them. And I'm trying to do my best on my own. It's a difficult task. It's very deceiving how difficult it is to write. You should know, obviously, from your own writing experiences.

**BB:** *What do you think of the art that's appearing in comics these days?*

**MO:** Actually, I think that's gotten better. I see a lot of artists now whose work doesn't make me puke. [*general laughter*] Even a lot of the guys who are copying other people's styles—like outright copying other people's styles—are still doing some good work. Because of the early '90s, when we had that crash, there were so many who were artists forced out of the industry. Unfortunately, a lot of good artists, too. I know some really, really talented guys who just quit during that time period. But it also got rid of a lot of people whose hearts weren't in it, and they were kind of just hacking work out. Or it made people reevaluate their work, like me. I wasn't strong enough during that time period to survive, so I had to reevaluate my work and come back with a different point of view.

So I think, right now, generally the art's a lot better than it's been before. There's definitely a greater variety of art, as well. You know, different types of artists, and people are more interested in seeing different types of art now. So I think I'm pretty excited when I go to the store. I'll pick up an issue of something I've never read before, or have never tried, in the middle of a story line and just to appreciate the art and see if I can learn something from it, because there are amazing guys out there right now.

John Cassaday, on *Captain America*, I look at that every time it comes out. I'm just like peeing on myself at how good it is. [*general laughter*]

**BB:** *Yeah, his* Planetary *work is breathtaking, too.*

**MO:** Yeah. Yeah, I'll look at a page of his stuff and go, "I suck!" [*general laughter*]

**BB:** *"And I mean that in the best of ways."*

**MO:** Oh, yeah. It totally makes me go, "Why am I drawing? Why bother?"

**BB:** *Would it be accurate to say that you like Will Eisner's new work, too?*

**MO:** Oh, absolutely. Absolutely.

Will is definitely an influence, too. That's my dream, to kind of be like Will Eisner. Not in the sense of his greatness, but in the sense of having been able to live as long as he has, and done as much as he has, and still be able to do new work.

**BB:** *And he's still thrilled about doing it.*

**MO:** Yeah! I met him last year at San Diego. He's just the nicest guy, and still excited to meet people, and that's what I hope for.

**BB:** *What kind of influence did Will have on your story-telling sensibilities, because I'd imagine they were fairly pronounced?*

**MO:** Oh, absolutely. And, again, with pacing.

One of my favorite books of his is *The Building*. Great story, great pacing. He's the master of the silent story, of being able to just show events happening. He was a big influence. I think Eisner's a great storyteller, and I learned a lot from him.

**BB:** *What do you think about Eduardo Risso, since you were talking about* 100 Bullets *earlier?*

**MO:** Oh, I'm a huge fan of Eduardo. I'm a huge fan of his work.

Recently, a friend of mine, Ivan, has been showing me some of Eduardo's stuff from France, some of his European stuff. And because it's in black and white, I like it even more. I think I'm even more with that stuff. He blows me away.

In fact, I hated him at first—because I was jealous. Like when I saw the first couple of issues, I was so overtaken by the work I felt a biting jealousy. Because I never heard of him before, I thought for sure this dude was like in his early twenties and he had just started out or something. It was a great comfort to find out he's been around for a while and he has some experience behind him. [*general laughter*] I was definitely feeling very petty, and very pitiful, when I first saw his work. It brought me to my knees.

**BB:** *The thing about Eduardo is that he reminds me of Eisner, not just in his sense of design and storytelling abilities, but even with, or because of, all this experience behind him, you can literally see him grow as an artist not just from page to page, but panel to panel. It's phenomenal work.*

**MO:** Absolutely. One of the interesting things he does is kind of like Eisner. You know, Eisner used to tell a lot of silent stories, and Risso does the same thing. A lot of times in the scripts, from what I understand, he'll get a script and it's about what's going on between A and B characters. But then Eduardo will pull the camera back, and start drawing a story about C and D characters, who aren't even involved in the main story. They're just background characters. But he makes them the foreground characters and tells a visual story about them, in silence, while the main action's going on in the background, especially if it's a talking scene. And that, to me, is really amazing.

And the fact that Eduardo and Azzarello are close enough that they can work like that is just great. And one of the great things about picking up *100 Bullets* is you get that feeling of family, of a family of creators who are simpatico, who are working on the same wavelength. The editor allowing them to have the freedom to do that. That's a great example of, I think, the great potential of comics and what books can be like at Marvel and DC.

**BB:** *Agreed. What do you think of Tricia Mulvihill's coloring on that book?*

**MO:** It blows me away. It absolutely blows me away, because it's able to maintain a pseudo black-and-white feel to the work. It's coloring, and there's, obviously, a whole prism of colors going on there, but it's not intrusive on the line work or the story.

I think that's one of the most horrific things about comics. Before bad writing, the first thing that will reject me is the colors. You know, you open up a book and it just looks like a Rubik's Cube exploded on it or something. It's just ugly, ugly colors. Big, bright, obnoxious, overdone computer coloring. So when somebody shows some reserve, it just stands up ten times better.

**BB:** *The thing is, that kind of oversaturation might actually work—if it was only used for certain kinds of effects that help support the story itself.*

**MO:** Yeah. Absolutely. And coloring can often be part of the story as well, and I think that's what Trish does.

I think that's one of the strong points about *Bastard Samurai*. Kelsey Shannon's coloring is like part of the story. And Kelsey can use really bright, psychedelic-like colors, but he knows how to use them in such a way that they're not repulsive in any way. They become like another character. And that's one of the things that I really admire about Kelsey's work, because I can't color at all. [*general laughter*] I have no color theory whatsoever. So, even when I see bad coloring, I don't know why it's bad, I just know that it bothers me. Same thing with writing. I'm learning more about writing, and like when I see bad writing I can't always tell you why it's bad, I just know that it bothers me.

And it's the same thing with coloring. I can't always tell why it's obnoxious and makes me want to throw the book out, it just does. And, unfortunately, there's whole companies like that. There are whole companies that demand their books be colored like crap. And they know who they are, so I'm not going to call them out. [*general laughter*]

**BB:** *Well, you say that you have no color sense, yet you mentioned that you've done watercolors in the past.*

**MO:** But watercolors have a life of their own, and often they will tell you what they're going to do, and what they're going to look like, without you having any choice in that. So it's just full of happy mistakes. [*laughter*] And, also, if I only use browns, you can't go too wrong. [*general laughter*] Just using some browns, varying shades of one color. I think that's the closest I'll ever get to coloring, is just varying shades of one color.

**BB:** *Well, what were you trying to do with the watercolors? Were you trying to do landscapes, or still lives, or something else entirely?*

**MO:** When I was learning my new style, I was basically just taking Frazetta paintings and then redrawing them in my cartoony style, and then watercoloring them. And people seemed to like it, and I was having a lot of fun. Actually, there's one piece that I did of *Powers* in watercolor. And I sold it to some guy for forty bucks or something. So there's one watercolor piece out there of *Powers*. I don't know where it's at, somebody has it.

**BB:** *What did those experiments do for you, and what did you get from it?*

**MO:** It brought in money, basically. [*general laughter*] eBay helped support me during the time I was working at the security job. I was drawing pieces that I would do for eBay at the job. So that I would get a check for seventy bucks for that weekend's worth of work, and then I would sell a piece for $100, $125 on eBay. So I like fooled myself that I was finally getting paid to draw. Of course, it was at the security job.

**BB:** *I actually know a few artists who are making a fairly good living just doing work that's destined for sale on eBay. It's almost like having a patron, in a sense, if you can work it right.*

**MO:** I tell a lot of artists that, who I know are struggling or that are trying to find work. I say, "Just do some pieces and put them up on eBay." You have to be careful about copywritten stuff, because some companies freak out. Some don't. But just do some naked chicks with swords and somebody will buy it, and then you can have lunch the next day. [*general laughter*]

**BB:** *Well, since you mention naked chicks, you just did a book called* 16 Naked Fairy Chicks. *What brought that on?*

**MO:** Well, I was going to do one of those little sketch-books for [Comic Con International] San Diego. I had a couple pieces, and some of them were nudes, and I decided I wanted to keep the nudes away from the other things so I didn't have to worry about who I was selling it to, I could just sell it to anybody. And just to keep it clean. So I took the nude pieces, and I had like three of them, and two of them for whatever reason . . . Well, actually, I know the reason. I'm a big fan of Brian Froud and Andy Lee, the guy who did one of the fairy books with him when I was a kid. It's just this book about fairies, and I've always just been in love with them, the whole idea of them, and the whole esoteric, Irish-Scottish folklore about the fairies. So those two pieces had fairies on them, and I figured "Well, why don't I make it a themed book?" So that's why I put the *Naked Fairy Chicks* book together. "Well, I'll just do a bunch more naked girls, and I'll just put wings on them." It was fun. It was goofy. I don't think we'll see it as a CrossGen book anytime in the future, though. [*General laughter*]

**BB:** *Will we be seeing more of this kind of work from you in the future?*

**MO:** No more naked fairy chicks. Yeah, I'll definitely do more sketchbooks in the future. But, as far as like a sketchbook, I kind of hope that, in the future, after I've done several projects at Image, to do an official sketchbook at Image that would feature everything from all those different projects I've worked on. But that wouldn't be for a long time, now.

**BB:** *Jumping back a bit, how did you approach doing the watercolors, and was this something you'd had a little training in before that?*

**MO:** No, I don't know anything about watercolors. I've just always been in love with them. I like it when watercolors bleed. I don't like it when watercolors don't look like watercolors. I've seen people use watercolors and I never would have known they were watercolors.

**BB:** *Right, they almost look like oils.*

**MO:** Yeah. Yeah, which is great, if that's what you're happy with. I like watercolors to bleed, and flower out, and to look like watercolors and have a life of their own. And when I do do a watercolor piece, and I haven't done one in probably like a year and a half to two years, closer to two years, when they work out, it's just so satisfying, because it's almost like gambling for me. Because I never took any watercolor classes, so I really don't know how to control it. So when it works out, it works out great. It's awesome. When it fails, well, then I have to throw the whole thing away, and that stinks. [*general laughter*]

**BB:** *How do you create one of those pieces? Do you start off with a sketch, or do you just have at it?*

**MO:** I'll draw the sketch first. And from the sketch, I'll draw it in pencil pretty tight, I'll paint it from there. I'll do the paints right on top of the pencils. And then, when I'm done painting, I'll go in with a pen or a brush, and then ink it on top. Because what I found out is if you ink it and then do the watercolors, often the ink becomes lighter because you've got layers of paint over them. Even if they're really faint watercolors, it still affects the outcome of it.

So that's how I usually do that. I haven't done it in a while, but I hope to do some more in the future, especially for *Hammer of the Gods*, maybe some pinups or something like that.

**BB:** *Do you think you might want to do the coloring that way at some point?*

**MO:** I don't think I'll ever do my own color book. I'm just talking about pinups, covers, that kind of thing. But, like I said, I have kind of a two-year plan. When those two years are up, hopefully I'll just be on *Powers* and doing *Hammer of the Gods* bimonthly, or like do two miniseries a year, something like that. And I'll have plenty of time to experiment more with watercolors, maybe take some watercolor classes. Take some drawing classes, even. For real, Steve Rude did that.

**BB:** *Oh, the reason I was chuckling was I'm thinking, "Yeah. Take some figure drawing classes, and we'll end up with another book of naked fairy chicks. Cool." [general laughter]*

**MO:** There you go! It'll be the Naked Chicks Sitting on a Stool book. Except they won't have implants. They'll all be real women, and nobody will want to buy it. [*more laughter*]

**BB:** *It really seems like you have a real capacity to continue to learn, explore new approaches, and apply them to your work.*

**MO:** Only if I'm interested in it. I'm actually a very terrible learner. I fact, I never finished high school. I was in high school and I was cutting class. And I was cutting class, not to do cool stuff like hang out and smoke cigarettes and get high, or get laid and play video games. I was staying home to draw, like a geek! [*general laughter*] But I cut class so much that they wanted me to repeat my junior year of high school. I was really pissed off. I was really pissed off, because I was passing my classes. Not with As or anything; I was a C and D student, sometimes a B in history, because I liked history. So I was passing my classes, but they wanted to keep me back just because they didn't feel I was there enough. And it really just pissed me off, so I was like, "Screw you," and I left, and I never went back. I went to go get my GED, but my high school was so crappy that I had never been introduced to half the stuff I needed to learn to get my GED. It would have been harder for me to get my GED than it would have been for me to just stay in school and pass classes. I needed to learn stuff that I had never heard of before, like trigonometry. My school, it was a regular high school, but to graduate you needed four years of gym, but only two years of basic math. [*general laughter*] But for my GED, I needed to learn trigonometry, geometry, and one of those other big words I don't remember. I couldn't believe that the standards were higher for my GED than it was for my actual degree.

**BB:** *That's a big statement about the basic standards of our education system, isn't it?*

**MO:** It is, it is!

But, at the time, I was sixteen or seventeen, and I knew it all. [*general laughter*] I had all the answers, so I was like, "Screw this, I'm going to deliver pizzas." So that's what I did. I started delivering pizza, and told myself I would give myself until the following summer to get a real job in comics, like a page rate job. If I didn't get one, then I'd go back to high school. I would repeat the year, just like I was supposed to. But that's when I got hired to do *Child's Play*, so I never went back. Which worked out fine for about ten years. [*laughter*] And then my career went down the drain, and I had nothing to fall back on.

It was very embarrassing to fill out applications. Not about my lack of a GED or diploma; that wasn't embarrassing, because nobody checks. Especially a security firm. All I had to tell them was that I was a licensed gun owner and they hired me right away. [*general laughter*] Not that I needed the gun, but I guess that was more impressive to them than a high school education. So, anyway, the thing that was embarrassing was never having any prior job experience. I was twenty-five, twenty-six, or twenty-seven, something like that, and I had to fill out a prior job section on my application and it was like, "Uh, nothing." [*laughter*] Or it would seem weird to say that I worked for Warner Bros., because DC is owned by Warner Bros., or to say that I was self-employed. And it was like, "What did you make last year?" I think, usually, on these job applications they would have a question asking, "What was your income for the last three years?" And it would be wildly bizarre. It would be like, "1994: $48,000. 1996: $3,000." [*general laughter*] And I thought for sure there was no way I would get a job, ever. Because, with no job experience, it seemed like I was completely lying about everything on there.

Luckily, I got a job. And that's when I could have used the high school diploma. But it didn't matter, because nobody checked! [*general laughter*] So there's your lesson, boys and girls. Just drop out of high school. Nobody will check. Don't worry about it. [*more laughter*] In fact, I'll be taking college courses at my local college relatively soon. I'll be taking some Spanish classes.

**BB:** *Just for the fun of it?*

**MO:**  Well, it's to learn Spanish, because my wife is Spanish, and we're teaching my son. And we hope to go to Spain, so I've got to learn. But I just find it ironic that I'll be going to college. And, of course, I'll eventually have to get my GED, because when my son's about sixteen and going, "Screw you, dad! Man, I ain't finishing no school, because you didn't finish it!" So I'll have to like write to *Rolling Stone* and get a degree. Maybe when I do that, I'll get a degree and become a cleric. I'll be like a father of my own church or something like that. [*general laughter*]

**BB:** *You said that you haven't had any real training in watercolors. Did you have any art training during your time in school?*

**MO:** In high school I had art classes but, you know . . . I love my art teacher, and no offense to him, but he wasn't teaching me the kind of art I was interested in, so I didn't learn anything there. I guess I learned a little bit about watercolors there, how to control them a little bit. I did the Art School of Minneapolis, Minnesota, it's an art correspondence school, and I learned some basic stuff from that. Some stuff that I didn't really apply to my comics, but it expanded my mind a little bit about art and stuff.

**BB:** *Well, obviously meeting Adam early on helped teach you a lot of what you needed to know.*

**MO:** Yeah. Most of my education came from going to conventions and meeting other comic book artists. Whether it was Adam, who I had met outside of the conventions, but then I had met Rich Rankin and Neil Vokes both, at a convention or through friends. Meeting guys like Rick Leonardi at shows, and corresponding with Mike Baron and Steve Rude through letters. And a lot of learning . . .

Ironically, you had said I seem to like learning, and I guess I do. But, again, it has to be about stuff I'm really interested in. I spent a lot of time at the library when I was younger. A lot of time reading stuff like mythology, in high school. Early years in high school I would spend a lot of time at the library reading books on mythology, Norse mythology especially, and art books. I spent a lot of time at the library. One of the most important things I learned from high school, because I think I can honestly say most of the things I learned at high school from books never applied in life, none of it, except for some minor math and my English skills, obviously. Which I eventually had to brush up myself later, to improve my own writing.

But really what I learned at high school was I learned how to learn. I think that's one of the most important things; if you don't teach yourself how to learn, then you'll never better yourself, or you will never get yourself fully educated. I think you can be in the worst school in the world, you can be in the worst ghetto in the United States, and still learn everything you could possibly need to learn if you have the motivation to do so. Unfortunately as a kid, I didn't have the motivation to do so. All my motivation came afterwards. Pretty much after I left high school, that's when I did most of my learning.

**BB:** *Who are some of the other artists whose work you really like these days?*

**MO:** Leandro Fernandez, he just did a *Queen and Country*. That's really, really good. Obviously, Steve Rude. He's still kind of a staple of the industry, and one of the guys I love.

I can't say there's a lot of new guys whose work I follow too much, but there are a lot of new guys whose work I admire. But that's just because I don't go out and read comics as much as I should. I don't get as much exposure to them.

I love what [Michael] Gaydos is doing on *Alias*. I think that's really amazing. I really, really love Jason Pearson's work. A relatively new guy, Rob Haynes, I love what he was doing. There's a whole new school of guys coming out with this sort of like cell animation feel to their work, you know, the monotone line weights and stuff. And I love that stuff. I can look at it anytime.

**BB:** *You said that you'd corresponded early on with Steve Rude. What were some of the things you learned from him?*

**MO:** He's great. He would take my photocopies and write notes all over them and send them back. And he'd draw on top of them, sometimes, to show me how to make characters more fluid, or how to make things . . .

Mostly, it was that. Mostly it wasn't so much about storytelling and things like that, it was mostly about keeping things more fluid. And then, reading about his own work through his sketchbooks where he'd talk about stuff like how to keep a page from becoming convoluted or cluttered, how to do your thumbnails . . .

You know, he literally draws his thumbnails the size of his thumb, and you can see the composition right there on the page. And that is a great way to simplify work. Steve was really great in teaching me about form, and structure of the body, and keeping things fluid.

I think one of my biggest influences, talking about Steve made me think about that, because of what I was saying about the fluidity and stuff, is just learning from animation. I had started studying a lot of animation. Like I got *The Iron Giant* on DVD, and a bunch of the Disney films, and just really paid attention to how their bodies are smooth and fluid, and how to use tangents—how to move the eye with the line work. A lot of cell animation is like that. It's just so instantly fluid and recognizable and conservative in its line. So I think that I learned from a combination of Steve Rude and animation.

**BB:** *That kind of design approach must really help you guide the reader's eye to the next balloon, or whatever you want them to focus on.*

**MO:** Definitely. I think that's one of those Eisner things. Eisner's always very good at directing the eye on the page, to tell you how to move things. You keep things moving from the left side of the page to the right side. Action almost always moves left to right. You don't always have to do that, because then it gets too rigid, but 90 percent of the time, you want that to happen. Things move left to the right. You keep the eyes about three-quarters of the way up on a panel, and that will leave plenty of room for word balloons, and it also helps create an invisible horizon from which everybody kind of hangs from, so the reader's eye will quickly move from one character to the next.

A lot of storytellers will swing their camera around, wildly, from one panel to the next. I'm not going to knock anybody for that, but I think that's one of the things that makes things confusing—other than composition. When the camera's moving around so much that you can't get a bearing on where things are, I think that makes things confusing for people. So that's why we have that kind of still camera, with repeated panels, a lot [in *Powers*].

**BB:** *It seems like you can use that kind of effect, where you do move the viewpoint around, but it really works best when it's tied into what's going on in the story. Otherwise, it's just like that bad coloring and becomes a real distraction, doesn't it?*

**MO:** Oh, absolutely. There are some artists who I absolutely love, and I really admire their work, but I can't read them visually. I look at the page and I can't tell what's going on.

**BB:** *Their visual narrative's broken up?*

**MO:** Uh-huh, absolutely. There are a lot of guys who have a very detailed look, and they're just so detailed that I can't tell what they're doing. One of Art Adams's strong points is that he's very detailed, but you can see things very clearly. His composition is strong enough that, no matter how much detail he puts on the page, you know exactly where to move and what to go to. But a lot of guys, they don't know how to do that. Sometimes I don't know how to do that. Sometimes I fail, especially on pinup images. Particularly if I have a lot going on in a pinup image. That's why usually my pinups and splash pages are very simple, because I have a tendency, if I have to do like a montage of images, to confuse it because that's one of the hardest things to do.

**BB:** *Do you think it's a different kind of spatial sense for you, having to go from panel-to-panel storytelling to the single images required by pinups, splashes, and covers? Almost like having to shift from using the right to the left side of you brain?*

**MO:** When you have the panels breaking up the page, it's very easy to dictate where the eyes are going to go. When you have a splash page, it's much more difficult. So one thing I've been doing is studying a lot of movie posters. A lot of times you'll see covers on *Powers* are analogous to album covers, movie posters, or book covers, and mostly it's because I'm learning as I'm doing. And I'm learning about composition from stuff like Russian avant-garde posters and stuff like that. I just did a series of covers for Oni, they have a new series called *One Plus One*, and I'm happy with those because I'm implementing a lot of that Russian sense of design. Which is almost like German Expressionism, but not quite as angular and as harsh. But there's definitely a sense of "This is where you go on a page, and how you look at things."

One of the other things I've really learned is, if you have a full page, you don't have to use the whole page. You leave large sections of it blank, and that allows for the images that are there to breathe, and to open up, and to move.

**BB:** *It sounds as if film has had an increasingly bigger impact on your work, mentally, if not visually. Who are some of your favorite directors, and why?*

**MO:** I think if any one film had a big effect on my work, it's definitely [Martin] Scorsese's *Taxi Driver*. The slow pacing, the slow reveal when there's something horrific around the corner, there's nothing more that I like to draw than somebody turning a corner to see something horrible. [*laughter*] You know, that really slow, painful pacing to then be opened up to something like, I forget what issue it was, but we had the guy from *FG-3* [the superhero team featured in *Powers: Supergroup*] exploding on the toilet. There's a couple panels of the other girl discovering the body, and it's just these slow panels of her looking, and then her eyes getting wide open, and then the double page splash of like the body with intestines all over the place. It's just horrific. And that comes from *Taxi Driver*. Scorsese just has that great sense of pacing and visual storytelling.

I think of the pages in *Powers* and *Hammer of the Gods* as being storyboards. I think of the pacing that way. A lot of comic book artists disagree with that. A lot of people say comics and film are completely different mediums, and I don't disagree with them. But that's just the way I choose to interpret it. And some people don't like that at all. They don't like *Powers* because of the repeating panels, or they don't like our taking our time and stuff. Which is totally cool. It's just the way certain people see books. It's their opinion.

But that's what I like about it. I like that kind of pacing.

**BB:** *Are there any other directors whose work you really like?*

**MO:** Yeah, there's definitely Fritz Lang. I like the German Expressionists a lot.

Mario Bava. I'm not a huge fan of horror films, but Bava's films are, I would guess, that they're one of Scorsese's strongest influences. In fact, anybody who likes Scorsese's work should check out *Black Sabbath* and, I think, *Black Sunday* by Bava. Just amazing frickin' films. He's got that slow kind of visual pacing to his stories, and comes up with some really, really great crazy images, and he uses the black on the screen amazingly. In fact there's a couple of scenes from *Black Sabbath*, which has three stories in it, and there's one about this vampire family in it. And there's a scene of Boris Karloff walking towards a house, and it looks so much like a Mike Mignola panel it just completely freaked me out. I was going to freeze and print it out and bring it over to him. That's how much his stuff just translates into comics. So, Bava I like a lot.

And there are other guys, too. I'm excited to see [Steven] Soderbergh's new film. I like his sense of storytelling, but I'm especially looking forward to his new version of *Solaris*, because I'm a fan of the director of the original film, [Andrei] Tarkovsky. This film he did about the Russian Revolution, or the sixteenth century, has got some of the most amazing visuals I've seen in it. Things you just visually don't expect to see. Not tricky camera work, just like really neat, bizarre images that are pretty profound.

I like symbolic images. You know, when something stands for something else and it's looming over you and you don't recognize it at first, until later on in the film. Then you watch it a second time and go, "Oh, wow, that is just rich with meaning." I think that's one of the problems with stories, both visually and on the page, is that they lack meaning. I think when something has meaning, that's when it becomes so strong.

**BB:** *Do you have an interest in doing storyboards for film, or otherwise becoming involved with the Hollywood scene?*

**MO:** Yeah. I definitely want to do some storyboards at some point. In fact, I was offered some storyboard work recently, and had to turn it down, because of schedules. But I definitely want to do storyboards at some point. I'm interested in directing short films, with some friends, just for the fun of it, because it's just another way of telling a story. But the little bit of experience I've had with making a film, it's a lot different than drawing comics, and it's a lot more difficult and a lot less enjoyable. [*general laughter*]

**BB:** *How do you approach writing, and how do you develop your ideas? Is it basically an instinctual process for you?*

**MO:** I've been writing most of my life. I haven't been writing for print until recently. I'd say the last four years I've really started studying more about writing. Brian's been helping me out a whole lot. Robert McKee's book on stories helped me out tremendously. Stephen King's book [*On Writing*] helped me out a whole lot. But just learning a lot from the Brians, both Brian Bendis and Brian Glass, has helped me out a lot.

For me, a story begins with the meaning or the idea. Mostly, it has to be the meaning. When I came up with *Bastard Samurai . . .*

Now *Bastard*, I only wrote the outline to. I wrote like a three page, two page, step outline, and I gave it to Miles Gunter, who I knew could really bring it to life, because I still didn't feel like, at the time, I was ready to fully write something. So that's why I invited Miles to help me out on it, and to bring his vision to the book.

For years, I had been a huge fan of *Highlander*. I just loved the visual image of modern-day guys fighting with swords, but I couldn't figure out why they would be doing that. I think that's a problem with a lot of comics now. Somebody will see something like *Highlander*, they'll want to do their own version of it, so they'll just do it, and they won't have a reason for it. I sat on the idea of guys fighting with swords for I'd say three or four years before I found a reason for it, like something that would make sense. And that's the modern-day samurai [idea behind *Bastard Samurai*]. So, once I had the meaning, then I could write the story around the meaning and everything else just falls into place around that.

With *Parliament of Justice*, I had some visual ideas, but once I found the meaning of the story, then it fell into place and I could write it very quickly. Because, once you have an idea of what the meaning is, all the scenes fall into place because of the meaning. It's like meaning dictates where things are going to go, and why things happen.

Same thing with *Hammer of the Gods*. Once I realized that *Hammer of the Gods* was about questioning your creator, it was about finding your creator, whether it's your father or God, and questioning them, "Why am I here?" or, "Why do you allow these horrible things to happen?" and then dealing with the consequences of that kind of arrogance, everything fell into place and the story was easy to tell from there.

So, for me, story always begins with meaning.

**BB:** *Have your scripts been growing in size and the details provided as you gain confidence in yourself as a writer?*

**MO:** Yeah. I think the closest thing I came to writing up to now was on *Hammer of the Gods*. I wrote a step outline for each issue and each page. I had trouble with the ending, and so that's why I brought Mark Wheatley in. So Mark took my step outline and then wrote a full script from it, and readjusted the ending so it would work.

**BB:** *What's your specific way of developing your ideas, once you've found that all-important central meaning, into an outline or script?*

**MO:** When I get an idea, I'll write down basically a large paragraph of the idea and the vague, vague, vague outline, and what the meaning is. And then it'll just sit around for a while until I feel like I need to tackle it, and when that happens, I'll write a step outline. Then, from the step outline, I'll create a page-by-page breakdown step outline. The dialogue is always last. It always comes last, because you have to think about . . . Well, for me, I have to think about, "What are the characters thinking about? What are their motivations?" and then that will dictate what they're going to say. So then dialogue becomes easier.

Dialogue, for me, is still difficult when I'm dealing with subject matter or people outside of my realm, outside of my class, outside of my educational background. Then it becomes more difficult. There are certain stories that I want to write, but I have no interest in writing the dialogue for, and that's when I bring other people on board. Sometimes I have to write everything myself, and sometimes I need help.

One of my favorite works that I've done, I don't know when it's going to be printed, I wrote it with my friend Ivan Brandon. I don't know when we're going to do it; it's probably going to have to wait until I have time to draw it, because I like it that much. And on that I guess I wrote 90 percent of it, and Ivan was heavy-handed with me with the editing and the dialogue. Ivan did a lot of research into the subject matter. We definitely worked together on it. It was like my first collaboration [as a writer].

The second thing I actually wrote the full script for is a project I have somebody else drawing right now. I don't know how long it's going to take for him to finish, so I'm pretty excited about it. But I'll wait until it's closer to being done [before I'll talk about it in detail].

**BB:** *That particular project, is that something else new?*

**MO:** Yeah. This one's different than the other ones I was telling you about.

**BB:** *Ah, so there's actually a number of things you've got going, but you won't talk about all of them at this point.*

**MO:** It's only because it's too early to talk about them. It's no big secret or anything bizarre like that, or some weird ego thing.

**BB:** *Oh, right. You just want to wait until the time's right before unveiling them.*

**MO:** A lot of these stories are just one shots. They're just forty-eight page, fifty-six page things, so it's not like I'm creating whole other series or anything crazy like that.

**BB:** *Right. The reason I'm digging a bit on this topic is that your two-year plan makes it sound like you wouldn't be doing this kind of thing in the future, but I figure that someone like you will always be doing something like these smaller projects on the side as you can fit them into your schedule.*

**MO:** Yeah. While I'm just also doing just the two ongoing books [i.e. *Powers* and *Hammer of the Gods*], I proba- bly also will be doing other stuff that I'm just writing and not have anything to do with the art. Unless I discover that everybody hates what I'm writing, in which case I'll abandon it.

Most of the stuff I'm doing is crime-oriented, though. I think that's just because of *Powers*, being exposed to it.

**BB:** *When you start putting things on paper, are you using a note pad and pencil, and then transferring that to a computer?*

**MO:** No, I almost always write directly into the laptop. Except for *Hammer of the Gods* stuff, because *Hammer of the Gods* usually comes to me at any moment, usually when I'm drawing or listening to music, like Led Zeppelin, and then I'll need to write something down in a notebook real quick. But, generally, I write right into a laptop, and I'll use Final Draft to write in.

**BB:** *Do you ever do any thumbnails or sketches to go with your initial writing?*

**MO:** No. No, I pretty much just let the story be the story at that point.

**BB:** *Just words.*

**MO:** Yeah.

**BB:** *That's interesting, because a lot of people seem to start out still writing it down with pen and paper before moving over to the computer.*

**MO:** Yeah, a lot of people do that. In fact, that's where most of my stories used to start out, with a pen, until I could afford to get the laptop with spell checking and all that. [*laughter*] What's great about the laptop is that I can send my outlines to friends and they'll say, "Well, this makes sense, but that doesn't make sense." You know, they'll help me out. While I'm confident of my writing, I want fresh perspective on it.

**BB:** *Hey, and when you can get some pointers and input from folks like Bendis, that would make quite a bit of sense.*

**MO:** Yeah. But still, you have to take people's suggestions . . . You still have to make your own decisions on what you're going to implement, and what you're not going to implement. Sometimes, that becomes the most difficult thing. But that's also, I think, why I like to let stories sit around and gestate. That way I can think about it.

**BB:** *One thing I've been wondering is, do you send your actual pages in, or just scan them and send them in electronically?*

**MO:** I pretty much, except for covers, I send all the pages in, just because they would take too long to scan in. If I was to do more of the work actually on the computer, then I would probably send the scans, but, at this point, I send everything directly to the letterer, and then he sends them to the colorist.

**BB:** *We talked about the coloring and how it can have a big effect on the art and the whole book. What about the lettering?*

**MO:** The invisible art.

**BB:** *Yeah, that's a fairly thankless job, isn't it?*

**MO:** Yeah, it totally is. It's a completely thankless job. I don't even like lettering on my art. [*general laughter*] Ken does an overlay, and that's largely just because of the way I work. Sometimes I don't like the lettering right on the art; I go right from the breakdowns to the inks, so it's not practical to have it done directly on the art.

But it's definitely a thankless job. It takes a lot of skill.

I don't mind computer lettering at all, it doesn't bother me. But hand-done lettering is just so much more human, obviously. It just comes across more . . . It doesn't feel so cold. And people just don't get to see what the letterer really does, or has to deal with.

**BB:** *What do you look for in a letterer?*

**MO:** Well, this goes back to the fact that it's a thankless job—I don't. I feel blessed on *Bastard Samurai*, because Ken is doing the lettering for me on that, and he's doing an amazing job. But if I had to settle for computer lettering, I would have been just as happy. But, looking back, knowing the job that Ken has done, I think he deserves a freakin' Eisner for what he's done. Because he didn't simply letter it, but he lettered it in such a way that it feels like the book. He adjusted his lettering style to something that fits into the context of the books, which you can't do with computer lettering.

But, at the same time, because it's the thankless job, it's kind of like being the bass player in a band. That job, it holds part of the book together. But, at the same time, if the bass player was replaced or something, nine times out of ten you don't know— unless he was a really good bass player. Same thing with a colorist, which is also a thankless job, not as thankless as lettering, but it's also a pretty thankless job. Colorists, they bring a lot of life to a book, but at the same time, it's pretty rare that they'll be able to change the impact of the book.

It's difficult to say, because it all depends on who's coloring, and who's lettering, and who really has control over those aspects.

**BB:** *It's interesting you bring this point up, because it really makes me think about those great letterers whose work it took me literally years to notice. People like Todd Klein, Tom Orzechowski, and workhorses like them.*

**MO:** Yeah, John Workman.

**BB:** *Yeah. These are guys who literally did everything from the logo designs that we all know by heart and don't realize it, to putting word balloons in characters mouths. What made me really notice this aspect was Klein's work on* Sandman *where, quite literally, his lettering helped tell the story. It moved the narrative, supported or supplied the mood, everything. And then there's Dave Sim and* Cerebus, *where the lettering literally can become part of the story itself in a real sense.*

**MO:** Yeah, yeah. Well, that's part of the ironic thing about computer lettering; while it's lifeless and dull, you have a level of control over it that you don't have over hand lettering. If you need to make changes to hand lettering after the fact, it's very difficult. It basically has to be done from scratch again. Whereas with computer lettering . . . If you look at Brian's work, for instance, in *Torso.* Some people hated his lettering, but I loved it. I loved his kind of pearl necklace design that he had, and he was really able to drag your eye around with it.

Same thing with Mack on *Kabuki*. He used computer lettering on *Kabuki* when he wasn't writing it with crayon. He used computer lettering, but he used the computer lettering in such a way that it was definitely part of the art.

**BB:** *Right. He deconstructed everything on that book.*

**MO:** Yeah. Yeah, that's hardly even a comic book so much as a codex or Rosetta stone or something, you know? [*general laughter*]

But, yeah, the letterer's job is definitely unappreciated, and not an enviable task.

**BB:** *Well, how did you get involved with* Footsoldiers? *It's one of those projects that you've worked on that is, in my opinion, like much of the work that Jim Krueger's done, sadly overlooked and underrated.*

**MO:** It's kind of a fairy tale thing. I was just at a convention in New York City at the time I was either doing *Judge Dredd* still, or I'd just finished it. I don't remember which one it was. And he came up to me at the show, and he was talking to me about this idea that he had. He had a whole bunch of people drawing his characters, and he had this great portfolio of stuff, and he had me do a pinup. And then he said, "I'd really like for you to draw this book." And then when he pitched it to Dark Horse, that's what it was, and that's just how it went.

It was great. It was one of the best work experiences I've ever had.

**BB:** *How did you two work on that book? Did Jim give you full scripts, or did you work from a plot?*

**MO:** Yeah, he had a full script. He lived, not completely close, but he was in North Jersey. So I would go up and see him, and there were times we would meet in New York and discuss ideas and designs and stuff. When I first started drawing it, we sat down for an evening and I designed all the characters with him. So he definitely designed his own characters, right over my shoulder, just saying, "Yeah, that would be cool. But what if so and so had this on him?" and stuff like that. So it was very cool.

**BB:** *Did you have much input into the story?*

**MO:** Not much. Also, at that point, I really wasn't even looking for input into the stories. That was the point where I was like a lot of comic book artists; I was just interested in drawing comics, and that was it. So I was content with just drawing it, trying to do my best drawing it.

**BB:** *Did you follow what he suggested in the script, or did you vary from that at times?*

**MO:** No, I drew exactly what it said to draw in the script. I was a good boy. [*general laughter*]

**BB:** *What were some of the other things about this project that made it so satisfying?*

**MO:** It was a good story. Even then, when I didn't recognize the difference between a good story and a bad story, I just loved it. It was nice and simple, and it was not a brain teaser, but it wasn't stupid. It was everything a fun comic book should be. You know, some comic books, like [Alan] Moore's stuff, have to be engaging, and have different meanings and different layers. And this was just like an old Jack Kirby comic book that was well written and very exciting. I just loved it.

**BB:** *Anything in particular you learned from Jim or working on that book?*

**MO:** I think, from Jim, there was some writing stuff that I learned from him. I learned how to implement certain storytelling techniques. I learned about the double entendre, which I think Jim is the master of. If you look at all his different creations there, they all have these great double meanings to them. And meaning is thick in his writing. You know, his characters mean something. The Second Story Kid, who tells tall stories and lies, and his boots elevate him, literally as well as figuratively, so his character is everything that his name implies. And he's got tons of characters and story ideas like that. It's a little heavy-handed, but it's great. I think it's perfect for comics. So that's one thing I learned from him, and it's great.

**BB:** *Yeah. I think Jim is, again, a really under-appreciated creator.*

**MO:** Totally. Yeah, I think if Jim would branch out more into the creator-owned stuff, he would set the world on fire all over again.

**BB:** *So you went from that to* Ship of Fools, *right?*

**MO:** I think so. Yeah, definitely, because I was moving from an apartment into a house. We were using the money left over from *Judge Dredd* and moving into a house, and I remember finishing up the last issue here at the house. And then desperately looking for work. [*laughter*] And that's why *Ship of Fools* happened, because basically nobody was offering me anything. I did little things, here and there, for Valiant or Marvel or DC, but little things, like pinups or three-page stories. I don't even remember. And that's when *Ship of Fools* happened.

Ship of Fools *was like* Hammer of the Gods, where it was just this daydream. It was all this stuff I liked and wanted to do. At the time, it was a combination of . . . I just always liked science fiction fantasies, like *Star Wars* and *Flash Gordon*. It was at the time when [*Reservoir Dogs* by Quentin] Tarantino had first come out, so there was lots of excitement about quirky storytelling. There was a lot of different stuff going on I was trying to jam all into one thing, so it was a lot of fun.

That was one of the best learning experiences in my comics history. I think that's where I really learned to tell a story. Even though it was all flawed, that's where everything came together for me, and then I was able to apply those lessons in some of my following stuff, *Bulletproof Monk*, and *Hammer of the Gods*, and then *Powers*. A lot of that goes back to *Ship of Fools*. In fact, I think you can see a progression in *Ship of Fools*. There's a trade that's really hard to find, that you can see a progression [in my abilities] from issue #1 to issue #6. And we plan on re-releasing it at some point in the future. Actually touching it up and completely fixing it and then re-releasing it at some point.

**BB:** *Similar to what Bendis did with* Fire, *then.*

**MO:** Absolutely. Yeah.

**BB:** *How did* Ship of Fools *come about, and what was the working process like on that one? Because you obviously had some influence on that story.*

**MO:** Yeah, definitely. The genesis of that started with a role-playing game. It was Adam Hughes, and myself, and Brian, and a handful of friends who lived nearby.

We'd get together and role played *Star Wars* basically, and had fun goofing around and eating pizza and stuff. I'd created a character there, and was in love with Tank Girl at the time. That's largely where the lead character, Marla, came from. She was me just wanting to do Tank Girl, and my fascination with Latino girls.

And I just melted all that together, and Brian and I created a few stories with the characters and different names and stuff. We just put together a story based on characters created from the role playing game, and my version of Tank Girl. I came up with this idea of . . . It wasn't really an idea I came up with, I was ripping off *Blake's 7*. Do you remember *Blake's 7* at all? [*general laughter*]

**BB:** *Yeah, as a matter of fact, I do. And it's funny you mention that show, because Greg Rucka has a real fascination with that show, too.*

**MO:** Oh yeah. Yeah, Greg and I talk about *Blake's 7* all the time. It's funny. In fact, I'm sure that Greg and I will get together someday to do our own rip off version of *Blake's 7*. [*more laughter*] But, yeah, I actually looked into getting the rights to *Blake's 7* for a while, and it was just impossible. So that's another part of *Ship of Fools*, it was me wanting to do *Blake's 7*.

So it was this kind of cliché idea of a band of outlaws who are forced to join together. You know, I guess I was guilty of writing and story crimes, myself, and *Ship of Fools* is full of clichés. Some of which I think is used well, because cliché is fine, I think, when it's used correctly. But we used it wrong a lot, too. [*laughter*]

But that's what it was. It was a lot of fun. It was just these ideas put together, and I had these really bizarre ideas at the time about how the universe worked, and Brian shared those ideas. We wanted a universe where anything could happen, like in *The Hitchhiker's Guide to the Galaxy*, or *Red Dwarf*, where just anything could happen. And, unfortunately, we had enough ideas that we were going to do 100 issues. [*general laughter*] Little did we know. By issue #3, we were barely breaking even, and we had to wrap it up really fast, and we did everything we could. So, hopefully, if we get to re-release it in the future, we'll be able to tell a little bit more of the story.

And Brian and I worked relatively close together, again. We just talked about the ideas. I just kind of created the characters; he created most of the story. I told him the things I wanted to happen in the story, and then he kind of put it all together. Like I gave him the ingredients to some sort of bizarre cake, and he baked the perfect cake for me at the time. We're happy with it, and proud of our flawed masterpiece. [*laughter*]

**BB:** *How did you get involved with* Bulletproof Monk*?*

**MO:** *Bulletproof Monk* happened because of this really little-known book that I did which, as long as nobody goes out and finds them, I'll tell you the title. It's called *Invisible Nine*, which was done through Image by this company called Flypaper Press. So I did this book, *Invisible Nine*, which is very cartoony and very goofy. I wasn't sure how to do a cartoony style, but I was trying to do it, and I was rushing through it because I was doing *Ninjak* at the same time. I was inking *Ninjak*, and penciling and inking this thing, *Invisible Nine*, at the same time. It gives you an idea of what was going on in my life.

The page rates were good, so it was cool. And, when that was done, they wanted me to draw *Bulletproof Monk*. So I did that, and I really liked martial arts stuff, so I was really excited about doing this martial arts stuff. So I did that. All I did on that . . . The writer actually designed a lot of the characters, because he was very in sync with a lot of that culture, the young, hip Asian culture. And I helped write the end of the story, like the end of the last issue. I just helped kind of restructure it slightly. But other than that, I just had a lot of fun drawing it, designing it, and doing research into kung fu. And that all became . . .

Flypaper Press and *Invisible Nine* were actually introduced to me because they were courting Brian at the time, when he was still doing *Jinx*. They wanted him to do a crime book for them, and it almost worked out where he and I were going to do a crime book together. But then it didn't come together, thank God. And that's how I was introduced to them, was through Brian.

**BB:** *Right, because you'd met Bendis a few years earlier, right?*

**MO:** Yeah, I met him at a comic book show, both him and David Mack, at the same time. And we hit it off, and just stayed in touch with casual phone calls and stuff, and then this thing with Flypaper started up and got us talking a whole lot more. And then, I had finished up *Ship of Fools*, and I called Brian and said, "Hey, I want to do this crime book with this wacky, cartoony style that I have," and that's how *Powers* got started.

**BB:** *So* Powers *came from that simple call, then?*

**MO:** Yeah, Brian and I were sharing ideas, faxing stuff back and forth. He would send me issues of *Jinx*, I would send him designs for stuff that I was doing, like a new series that Brian Glass and I were coming up with based on Quixote, which we're turning into a novel which I'll illustrate at some point in the future. So I was sending him pages of that, and other stuff that I was doing. So we just kind of knew that, eventually, we were going to end up working together. And, when *Ship of Fools* was done, I wanted a complete change from *Ship of Fools*, because I had just spent a year and a half to two years [on it]. We had gone from failing at Caliber to failing at Image. [*general laughter*] So it was a long haul, and I was looking to do something completely different, and especially get away from science fiction for a while.

And I wanted to try the crime stuff, so I called up Brian and said, "Hey, we're all done. If you have any ideas, you want to work on something?" And he was like, "Oh, that sounds great!" So I faxed him over some stuff that I had in mind. I guess about a week later he sent the outline for *Powers*, and this thing called "Who Killed Retro Girl?" And I was like, "I don't know if I want to do this. It's got superheroes in it. I'm not really interested in drawing superheroes." And he was all, "Aw, it has nothing to do with superheroes. Trust me, man, it's all crime stuff. There's just some superhero stuff in it, but it's all in the background, totally." [*general laughter*]

**BB:** *"It's all bait and switch, baby!"* [*more laughter*]

**MO:** So, they were going to do it in black and white, because that's what we were working in at the time, we were both doing black-and-white stuff. And then

Brian says, "Well, I want to try this in color." And I was like, "Oh crap! I was going to make a living!" Because, in black and white, you can break even at 2,500 copies, and Brian had built up enough of an audience that we could have done the book at like 4,000 copies an issue. Which meant that I could have made almost a $1,000 a month, which, with my week-end job at security and doing that during the week, that would have been great. I would have been making a living and paying my half of the bills and all that. And then Brian screwed it up with wanting to do it in color, and I was just like, "Aw, man, this is just impossible. We're just shooting ourselves in the foot."

But I was told to go along with it, and totally being hopeful. And then the numbers came in for issue #1, and they were just above break even. And we were both kind of like, "Oh, this stinks!" And then Image, the brain masters there, they're just great, man. They came up with this idea; they double-shipped issue #2 to people. That's why issue #2 is so hard to find, because they only ordered like 10,000 copies or something just under break even. I don't know what the numbers were, but they were really low. So they double-shipped us out and, all of a sudden, people saw issue #1 and everybody had issue #2, and it was like, "Wow, this is a good series." And the numbers for issue #3 came in, and they jumped up like five or six thousand copies.

And then our reorders were breaking records, reorder records at Image, and it was just reordering like crazy. And then issue #4 numbers came in, and they were good enough that . . . I think it was between issues #4 and #5 that I quit my weekend job and was able to work full time on *Powers*. It was amazing. And our numbers just kept going up, and kept going up. And now we're kind of at an area where it slowed down, but our numbers still peak every now and then, so we're still growing. So we basically have seen steady upward numbers from the start, and it's just incredible. The trade came out, and we're into the third printing of the trade now, and it's been just incredible.

**BB:** *All of which has really allowed you to concentrate on the two things that really mean something to you, your family and the work.*

**MO:** And then I had to screw it up by taking on ten other projects! [*general laughter*]

But, to be fair, I had actually started *Hammer of the Gods* before I started *Powers*. I started that before *Powers*, not knowing if anybody was going to publish it. I think the first issue was drawn already, and I hadn't even gotten in touch with Mark Wheatley yet, because I didn't realize how much trouble I was in with the story. [*laughter*] So, I had done four issues of *Hammer* before we solicited it. It was originally only going to be four issues, but then we decided the last issue would be issue #5, because we had just run out of room.

So I hadn't drawn *Hammer* in quite a while, because 90 percent of the work was done. "I've got forever to do the last issue. I don't have to worry about that, I'm way ahead on *Powers*," blah-blah-blah. Then I get the call from Graffiti [Designs] to do Kevin Smith's *Bluntman and Chronic*. And it was just too good of an opportunity to turn down. So I agree to do that, and then the schedules started colliding.

It was like a freakin' car accident on the highway. It was just like, "Bam-bam-bam!" And then, eventually, it got so bad, because Kevin was filming [*Jay and Bob*] *Strike Back* at the same time, so his scripts were late. They started out on time, but then his own schedule was conflicting with the comic book schedule, because he was filming a frickin' movie. Which is a pretty big deal. So that means the script's late, and that changed the original schedule I was on. So then *Powers* and *Bluntman and Chronic* started to conflict. And then, that last issue of *Hammer* was finally due. You know, the one that I had so much time to work on, because, you know, I had done 90 percent of the work, I was way ahead on *Powers*, and I don't have to worry about it? And that's when everything hit the fan.

There were two months there where I was penciling and inking *Bluntman and Chronic*, penciling and inking *Powers* monthly, penciling and inking *Hammer of the Gods*. *Hammer of the Gods* was due immediately. *Powers* was due immediately. And so was *Bluntman and Chronic*, because the second Kevin was done with it, it was going to go out and ship. Because it was going to be one issue now, not three issues. So that meant that instead of having to have one issue's worth of stuff done at the original deadline, I now had to have three issues worth of stuff done at the original deadline, because it was a graphic novel now, instead of just three issues. Whereas if it was just three bimonthly issues, it wouldn't have been that much of a problem. But, in order to time it with the film, we had to bump it from three bimonthly issues to one graphic novel, so all that work had to be crunched down into this one time period.

So it all became a huge nightmare, and that's when *Powers* became late. For a while there, for almost a year, *Powers* was like anywhere from six to eight weeks late per issue, which is just terrible. Sometimes we would get it out in a month, but it was just a real nightmare. I was going insane. I had no time for anything. My mind was just blowing up. That was when I called in Neil to help out with a lot of the projects, and Kelsey Shannon helped out with issue #5 of *Hammer of the Gods*, as well. I just needed help with it because things were way out of control.

And then I started to get things under control again, after both *Hammer* and *Bluntman and Chronic* were done, and just as I was starting to get caught up with it, my mom got sick. She fell really, deathly ill. She almost died. We actually gave her last rites. She was in the hospital with blood in the tubes and everything, it was just terrible. So then I lost a month's worth of work, there. Just as I was starting to get ahead, this disaster comes and throws everything back again.

So I'm just now, from this chain of events, I'm just now recovering from last—I guess it was last year, starting with the *Bluntman and Chronic* thing. So it's taken this long to get ahead from there. And it just wasn't one thing, it was several projects on top of each other, with circumstances that were unforeseen, that threw me into this craziness.

Which is one of the reasons why I've decided not to solicit anything until it's finished. That's why I'm really only talking about *Parliament of Justice*, because that's all done. And *Nevermore*, I'm not going to solicit that until I'm done. So I'm sticking really close to that rule, so that unforeseen things will not destroy my schedule in the future. [*laughter*]

In other words, I'm learning to just slow down in general. Because one of the things I wanted to do was to solidify a place for myself in the industry, so that, while *Powers* is going on, I'll be known for something else other than just *Powers*. That way, when *Powers* does finish up, then people will expect more from me. And I think I've created enough projects for myself, from when I've started *Powers* to the next two years, when I'll be done with some of these other projects, to have done that safely and to be able to take a break and draw just *Powers* and *Hammer*. To only draw two books! [*general laughter*]

**BB:** *Except for the occasional graphic novel or one shot on the side.* [*more laughter*]

**MO:** Well, no more graphic novels, either. That was something I learned from *Bluntman and Chronic*. Which was a lesson that I learned from Adam Hughes from when he did *Star Trek*. He sat me down on his knee one morning and said, "Mike, listen up. Don't you ever draw a graphic novel. Because you spend the amount of time it would take to draw three or four issues of material for one book that comes out and then it's in people's eyes and out of their hands as quickly as one single issue. So you're putting three to four times the amount of work on something that people are only going to spend as much time as they'll spend looking at a single issue." So, a graphic novel is kind of a waste of your time. Unless it's a really, really short graphic novel.

**BB:** *Or it's a collected edition of single issues.*

**MO:**  A collection afterwards, yeah. But never again will I do like a ninety-page graphic novel. A forty-eight-page one shot is OK, because it's too long to be just two issues worth of stuff. But never a graphic novel again. Because you put a lot of time into something people are only going to pay attention to for a week.

**BB:** *Ideally, that would change somewhat in the future with the bookstore market opening up, but I can see your point as far as the direct market and comic shops are concerned.*

**MO:**  Yeah, because with *Bluntman and Chronic*, everybody talked about it the week it came out, and then, that was it. Whereas *Powers*, or any other thing that I've done that's miniseries or whatever, even *Hammer of the Gods*, which was hugely less successful than *Bluntman and Chronic*, people talk to me about that a lot more, because there's so many more issues of it. There's more of it versus a one-shot deal. It's kind of like the difference between having a one-night stand and having a relationship with somebody.

**BB:** *What was it like working with Kevin Smith? Was it enjoyable, despite all the delays and pain?*

**MO:** It was fine. We worked basically through e-mails. He sent me a couple of nice e-mails about the art, welcoming me onto the book, stuff like that. But generally he was out of contact, because he was filming and I was incredibly busy, drawing too many books at once. So he was cool. And he was very hands off, and he let me do what I wanted to do, and I appreciated it.

We swore an oath to hook up at some point, but we keep missing each other at conventions and stuff like that. I'm sure one day I'll finally get to meet him. So, yeah, it was fine

**BB:** *Were you working from a relatively full script, or plot outlines on that?*

**MO:** They were full scripts, but they were very vague. They were heavy on the dialogue, but he didn't give a lot of direction, which was cool, because it let me kind of do what I wanted. I mean, the direction was there, but it wasn't really tight.

**BB:** *OK. Almost like a play script, then.*

**MO:** Yeah. Very loose. And I think it was the funniest thing Kevin's ever written. I was very happy to be part of it. It was a lot of difficulty, and I complain about it a lot because of my scheduling at the time, and whenever I think about it, I think about the hard time I was going through drawing it, but, in retrospect, it was a lot of fun and I'm very proud to be part of it.

**BB:** *Well, with* Powers, *you developed that with Brian from the ground up. Was that a process almost like what you had with Jim, where he was kind of looking over your shoulder, or was it looser than that?*

**MO:** Not visually. Basically, I would fax designs to him. Like, when we designed Retro Girl, I originally had a much more gaudy costume, but it was basically the same costume. So I would send him the design, the gaudy design, and he would say, "Well, take the lightning marks off, do less of a Wonder Woman look to it," or something like that, or, "Move the thingie," that infamous "thingie" that we always say. So I'd change the thingies, and then, that was it. And that was kind of it on everything.

I think the only major design change was Deena. I had originally wanted to draw her with either black hair or red hair. I don't even remember anymore. But she looked too much like Walker's sister. It just didn't work. Walker was always Walker. Walker always looked like that, there was no change to him, other than I was drawing his chin a little too big originally, in the sketches.

But, generally, I would design things and fax them to Brian, and he would just give me some minor feedback, and badda-bing, that was it. So Brian lets me do what I want, visually, but he's always there to be with me.

**BB:** *What about story generation?*

**MO:** Up to this point, it's mostly been Brian. But I've had some suggestions for stories and stuff like that that he's taken to, so we'll do some of that stuff in the future. I think, initially, he's got a lot of really strong ideas that he wants to tackle. And even my ideas that I'll come up with, I won't be writing scripts or anything like that, it's more just conceptual ideas.

**BB:** *Like, "Brian, what if . . ." and then let him run with it?*

**MO:** Yeah. Why change the way our creative process works?

**BB:** *You've said that you learned a lot about pacing from Brian. Is there anything else you might have learned from him?*

**MO:**  Well, one of the other things I learned from him was about marketing. About marketing yourself, how to present yourself in public, when you're at conventions.

A good example is I would apologize for myself. When I was at a convention with him, I would drive him crazy, and Neil would point this out to me, too, saying, "Never apologize for the work you've done." Because often, if I had done a sketch for some-one and I didn't like it, I wouldn't charge the person, or charge them less, or apologize to them. And Brian would point out to me that, both at conventions and when you're talking about your own work, whether you're talking about a trade paperback or anything, you don't want to point out the flaws in your own work because people might not have noticed it other-wise. And that's not a trick or anything like that, it's just . . .

An example was he was watching a film that had commentary on it, and he loved the film—until the filmmaker pointed out a major flaw in the plot or something. And it did ruin it for him afterwards, or it lessened it for him, because he then realized, "Wow, that did kind of suck." [*general laughter*]

So, that was one of the things: just present yourself with pride. Whatever mistakes you made in your work, just deal with it, and realize that's part of it. If somebody else points it out, that's fine, agree with them, but don't go ahead and apologize for it beforehand.

There was stuff like that, and the idea that, if you're presenting your work, be proud of it. Be proud of what you've done. Also, there's a difference between hyping yourself, and promoting yourself, and you have to find that line. Hyping yourself is when you wear your own T-shirt to a convention. Promoting yourself is when you have your books and you're pushing them to people. Hyping yourself is when you dress up as your character, in costume; that's also very tacky. [*general laughter*] I guess that's the difference. Hyping yourself is tacky. Promoting yourself is business.

So anybody who wears their own character costume to a show, or hires somebody to dress up, every time I look at that, I just cringe. But that's just me. [*laughter*]

**BB:** *That's a very valid point in many cases.*

*You mentioned one of the things that makes Brian such a good writer is his sense of pacing. One of the other things he is known for is his dialogue. What makes Brian's dialogue so good, and is that really another of his strengths, in your opinion?*

**MO:** Brian is always thinking about writing. When Brian is arguing with his wife, he's taking mental notes.

[*general laughter*] When Brian is at the mall, and he's dealing with some stupid petty high school dropout like me behind the counter, you know, like, "Uh, I don't know, uh, where DVDs are?" He's taking notes on stupid people arguing, or smart people arguing, or why people think a certain way, or when he's watching the news. He's always taking notes. In fact, there was one time when his life was in danger, and he was taking notes!

I hope I'm not stealing one of his stories, but he's told this plenty of times. One time he was taking photo reference for either *Jinx* or *Torso*, I think it was *Jinx*. He was in Cleveland, out on some bridge with some friends, taking photos, and he had a plastic gun. And somebody called the cops. So, when they showed up, and I believe this story's correct, the cops pulled their guns out on them, because they knew they had a gun on them. Now, I don't think Brian had the gun in his hand or anything like that, but basically the story goes that they weren't arrested, but the cops gave them a good talking to. And Brian was apologizing to the cops, saying, "I'm very sorry, sir." And one of the cops said, "Don't apologize to me. I wasn't the one going home in a body bag." And Brian, of course, is thinking, "Oh, thank you for the dialogue!" [*general laughter*]

So that's what makes Brian's dialogue so good. He keeps track of what people are saying, and why certain people say these things. So that's one of the things.

The other thing is Brian studies his craft. A lot of writers don't do that. A lot of writers write because they've read a million books, so they've kind of subconsciously picked up on the rules of writing. But Brian, he studies. He understands back structures and why they work, and beats, and all that technical crap. There are no rules about writing, but there are guidelines that will help you become a better writer, and he's spent time writing and studying that.

And people point out his dialogue, which I think is great, but I think it's more Brian's ideas that are better. His idea of what is the story about? The media aspect of *Powers*, that's what *Powers* is about. It's not about Walker or Deena or how fast they can run down an alleyway or them jumping over cars or how many dead bodies they can find or whatever. It's really about how people react to that world. And people don't realize that's what makes it special. And that's why the other . . .

There are other *Powers* knock-off books, not a lot of them, but books that have definitely been modeled after it. And the good ones get it, and the bad ones don't. And even the things that a lot of them are imitating, things we are doing in *Powers* have been done before. We're not really doing anything new. We're just presenting it, I think, in a unique package.

The whole "superheroes through the eyes of cops" thing has been done plenty of times before, and it's been done plenty of times after.

So I think that's what makes Brian a good writer. That, and he knows how to steal from [David] Mamet without anybody knowing it. [*general laughter*] Only kidding, Brian, only kidding.

**BB:**  *So how'd you develop* Bastard Samurai?

**MO:**  Well, that was me ripping off *Highlander*. [*general laughter*] Like I said, the initial gestation of the idea came from *Highlander*, from just loving that visual of guys in modern days fighting with swords. Unlike 90 percent of the comics out there, which are about girls fighting with swords for no reason, I at least found a reason for people to be fighting with swords. [*more laughter*] And that's the thing I'm most proud of with that book, was I found a reason for people to fight with swords in modern days. That was from my love of samurai films. I had seen *Ghost Dog*, which is a film I love a lot, but when I went to see it, I was expecting something different. And that's what gave me the idea of using the samurai aspect, to marry that with *Highlander*. Kind of like samurais meet *Fight Club*.

So, once I had that, I found the meaning. The meaning for me was about the truth. It was about being lied to all your life. A lot of people have had family secrets in their lives, or they've been told things about life which they later find out are wrong, or to be a lie, and they want to change it, but they can't. But in this case, instead of rules which teach him that, "Well, you can change it," in the Bushido code of samurais it's a thing called rectitude, which is "the righting of wrongs."

So he finds out that he's not a samurai, that he's been lied to all this time, that they're just being used as modern-day gladiators for fighting. And he goes on his journey of rectitude—which is not the same as revenge. Revenge is an emotional thing, "an eye for an eye." This is the righting of wrongs. He was righting the wrong by erasing the schools, by destroying them. So that's what that book's about.

**BB:** *Did you start out this miniseries with a loose outline, as you did with* Hammer?

**MO:** Yeah. A lot of times, I'll start out with a loose idea for something. I'll have an outline for something, but I don't know what it's about yet. So stories, for me, start one of two ways: they start with an idea, or they start with a meaning. Either way, they can't go forward without the meaning being there. In fact, one story I have, I only have the act structure. I know a neat way that's set to tell this story, but I don't have the story yet. I just have the act structure. [*laughter*] So, once I find the story in the meaning, then I can proceed with it. But, if I don't know what it's about, I'm not going to try to write it.

What I found fascinating when I was listening to Stephen King's book, *On Writing*, he writes the opposite. He'll find the characters and the "what if" factor, and then he starts writing from there. Then he discovers what it's about as he's writing, which I found completely fascinating, and a big leap of faith in your own ability to write.

**BB:** *And dangerous, too. You could get a couple hundred pages into something and discover it's not really about anything, and without any real direction.*

**MO:** Yeah. I think that's where a lot of writer's block comes from. I think that's why a lot of writers get frustrated, because they don't know what it's about. I'm not saying that's bad. That's not a bad way of writing. But writing that instinctually can be dangerous, and can lead you to a wall where you just don't know what's going on.

**BB:** *When you're writing for somebody else, do you worry about how they draw, or are you more concerned with just getting what you see down on the page?*

**MO:** Only Neil. When I wrote *Parliament of Justice*, I knew that it was for Neil, and that's the only time that I've—not that I write a whole lot—but that's the only time that I've written something specifically for some-body else and their temperament. That's why I didn't write any dialogue. It was like a really loose outline of every page. Well, it wasn't that loose, but like I said, I'm pretty sure it had panel breakdowns. Because I knew he is very demanding in his work, of doing things a certain way, of the way he expresses himself in his work and the process of the work, so that I definitely wrote for him.

But everything else, I pretty much write for myself, and then I find other artists who are willing to work within those boundaries. And if they're not, then they don't have to do the project, and it's not a big deal. I'll just wait for somebody else, or I'll do it myself. Generally, I just kind of write for myself. Like, what do I want to see, what do I want to read about.

**BB:** *How happy are you with the results of* Bastard Samurai? *Do you feel like you've accomplished every-thing you set out to do?*

**MO:** I think so. It's a scary thing to say, because it took on a life of its own. And I'm very happy to have brought on Miles, especially. I think Miles Gunther is going to be a big writer in the future, I really do. I really think when he's exposed properly, he's going to be influential, because he's got such great vision to his writing. Especially the visuals. He's able to marry the visuals with the script. He describes things very visually, without being intrusive.

And, yeah, we accomplished pretty much everything we had in mind with *Bastard Samurai*. I'm really happy with it. And shocked, because I was afraid that people were going to be lost with it, because we decided our number one rule was to do no outright exposition. There's exposition in there—everything needs exposition whenever you have fantasy—but it's not captions explaining to you what's going on. Everything you find out about the story, he was able to do either visually, or through dialogue, and, again, without it sounding like somebody's explaining to you everything that's going on.

You can't just read *Bastard Samurai* while you're watching TV, like you can with a lot of comics. And that's not a dis on those comics that you can read half paying attention to, because a lot of my favorite comics are like that. *Hellboy*'s kind of like that. You can read *Hellboy* while your kids are running around, or something like that. So a lot of books I like, you don't need to have full attention on. But *Bastard Samurai* left a lot for the reader to fill in. We still get some people who just weren't sure what was going on, but 90 percent of them loved it.

So I'm very happy with the way it turned out, and Miles and I will be working together again soon in the future. Hopefully, me, Miles, and Kelsey will work together again. Yeah.

**BB:** Hammer of the Gods *has really turned into a major success, something, like* Powers, *that most creators dream about doing once in their careers. And here you've got both going on simultaneously. When you brought Mark on board, did that help kick it up a notch in any real sense?*

**MO:** Oh, absolutely. Obviously to anybody who's read *Breathtaker*, he's a great storyteller. He is a very good writer. He's a very different kind of writer from Brian. Which is good. I don't know how to describe the difference between the two, but what I think is most important is they both have a very strong understanding of meaning and story. Now, the way they go about expressing that is different, but that's cool. I think Mark is a more traditional comic book writer. But, again, they're both very centered on structure and meaning and what's the story about.

The other thing that Mark could offer was that I knew he had some good knowledge of Norse mythology, himself. Plus all the production work that he could do on the book, so I wouldn't have to concentrate on anything but the art. So he's very respectful of my wishes on what I want to do on the book, while at the same time able to offer new things to the series. We really make a good team together, and he's definitely a full cocreator on the book, not just a hired writer.

I'm really happy with both series. And if I could just get certain stories out of my system that I feel like I need to do and I need to tell, then I'll be able to just concentrate on *Powers*. And *Hammer* comes so easily, I could easily do both books at the same time without it being a problem. And I'd be extremely happy.

**BB:** *Have you and Mark continued working the way you did on the first* Hammer *arc? You come up with the basic plot idea, and then you two pass it back and forth until you're both happy with it?*

**MO:** Yeah. On the next miniseries there was a lot more back and forth than the first one. For the first one, the outline—which he expanded, to allow more things to happen, to make it grander—was followed pretty closely. Because I probably would have had it being a little tight, which would have left out some of the grand effect of being in Asgard, and fighting giants, and the big, open images.

On the second one, *Hammer Hits China*, there's a lot more back and forth on. Because I wanted to introduce some of my interest in kung fu, Chinese mythology, and martial arts, and, at the same time, keeping it focused on Norse mythology. So there was a lot more back and forth on that, and we just worked really well together because we can be honest with each other. I can tell him, "I just don't like this," or, "I just don't want to do that," and he has no problem with it. He's totally cool. There are no egos involved, because we know each other and trust each other, which is as difficult a job to create or put together as creating a book. Finding someone you can trust and work with that well is hard work.

**BB:** *What's the process of coloring the first mini been like?*

**MO:** Mark is working with John Staton, and together they're creating a style of coloring that I've honestly— outside of *Fafhrd* and the *Gray Mouser*, and it's even different than that—I've never seen it before. It's a combination of computer and kind of a painted look. It kind of looks to me like rough Frazetta paintings. And he's just created a coloring style that just excited me so much that, after seeing it, that's when I decided I eventually just wanted to do *Powers* and *Hammer of the Gods*.

Because, before that, I was going to do this next miniseries of *Hammer of the Gods*, then there was going to be one more large miniseries of *Hammer of the Gods* called "Birthright" that would be about nine issues, and then that would have ended the series. But I liked what he was doing so much, and it's brought such another level of daydream reality to it, that I want to continue doing it.

**BB:** *John's really turning into something, isn't he?*

**MO:**  Yeah, he colored the online strips that we did, which were much more bright and traditional. Especially for the Internet, because it worked so well in that format. But the way he's working with Mark right now, it's definitely more earth tones and this painted look.

John's a great colorist and artist in his own right. Hopefully we'll get to see his book soon. I don't know if you've seen any of the work he's done. He's definitely a manga artist, and he does incredible work. Hopefully,  he'll get so busy and successful one day that he'll have to stop coloring my books and he'll be busy doing his own.

**BB:** *Do you think that* Hammer of the Gods, *like* Powers, *is something that we'll eventually get to see on the big screen?*

**MO:**  It's possible. There's  a screenwriter we were approached by, from CAA, which is a pretty big agency in Hollywood for screenwriters and actors and such, who wants to adapt it into a screenplay.

**BB:** *Do you think that would be live action or animated?*

**MO:** Probably live action.

**BB:** *Do you ever play those "casting the flick" kind of mind games?*

**MO:** I would just want a good actor. And for *Powers*, I just want a really good actor. You know, people are talking size and people were thinking about big guys first. For me, I'm just thinking about good actors first.

I think with *Hammer*, you kind of do need a larger guy. But that's impossible to find. A big, large guy who can act well is a really difficult thing to find. Maybe there's a wrestler who can secretly act for *Hammer*, I don't know.

But, for *Powers*, Tom Hanks could play Walker. I think he'd be great, because he's a great actor. Or Brad Pitt, I think he's a great actor, too. I guess George Clooney would be my first pick. In other words, it doesn't really matter to me, the physicality of the person. It has to be a good actor who can bring something to the role. For me, that's what's important.

**BB:** *You said earlier that you'd like to direct small films. Would you ever want to direct something larger than that, you think?*

**MO:** Well, I'm open to anything. But it's very difficult. It's not the same.

When I'm drawing a comic, the reaction and the set up and the results are instantaneous. Well, almost instantaneous. It's a couple of hours and—Bam!—it's finished, whereas with film, it takes forever. And you don't know what the heck you're shooting, and you don't know how it turned out until you look at it, later on. I definitely want to try more of it. But it's definitely harder, and it's not where my true love is, but I definitely want to try it more.

I would like to eventually direct one actual film. It doesn't have to be a big film, but an actual, ninety-minute thing, at some point in my life. But no time soon. [*general laughter*]

**BB:** *One of the things we've kind of talked around, even when speaking about Mark and John, is the fact that you're part of the Insight Studios Group.*

**MO:** Sure. I'm like the fifth Beatle. [*general laughter*] I'm an associate, I guess that's the best word.

**BB:** *What does that kind of affiliation offer you?*

**MO:** It's really started with *Hammer of the Gods*, obviously, and it's really just about working with good artists and production team. And Insight's been doing comics, as a production company—they've been publishing in the last couple of years, especially with Frank Cho's work—but, obviously they've been around for over ten years of doing incredible stuff. I've got to finish up this thing called *Dr. Cyborg* eventually for them, which is a daily online strip. I think I've got like thirty more days of strips to finish on it. That's a little late for a daily. It's about a year late. But, eventually, I'll finish that up.

Working with Insight is the icing on the cake of getting to work with Mark.

**BB:** *What have you learned from Mark? He's another one of those guys who is just incredibly undervalued and criminally overlooked, and certainly one of the most fascinating conversationalists in the entire field.*

**MO:**  Mark is incredibly intelligent. He's like hyperintelligent. It pains me to be around him sometimes, because I just feel like ten times dumber than I am. He's just incredibly interesting. He's got a million stories. And he and his wife have done tons of stuff. Like, she's very much into digging up bones and history and stuff like that. You go over to their house, and they've got a ton of books, and they're really interesting people who have just done a ton of stuff.

I really like hanging out with Mark. Mark's a completely honest person. I totally love him and have a great time hanging out with him. And I've learned a lot about production stuff and design work from him, as well.

**BB:** *Anything in particular that sticks out in your mind?*

**MO:** Honestly, all that stuff is completely foreign to me. All I know is Mark is a master of it. [*laughter*] Yeah, that's all I know. [*general laughter*]

Mark knows how to put a book together. He knows everybody at Diamond. He knows all printers. He knows foreign printers. He knows everything about foreign book deals, all kinds of stuff. I mean he's a publisher, an artist, and a production house, all wrapped up into one person. And he's got a vast wealth of knowledge.

**BB:** *Do you have much of an interest in publishing yourself? You obviously had something to do with the* Naked Fairy *book.*

**MO:** [*laughter*] Not really. That's stuff I really don't want to know about.

Actually, that's one of the things I'm weakest at; promoting my own work when it comes to putting ads together, or any of that stuff. I just draw the page. I don't want to really deal with putting the book together. That's too much trouble for me. [*general laughter*]

**BB:** *Well, I know that you're really committed to doing your own stuff, but is there a book or certain characters that, in your secret fanboy heart of hearts, you'd love to have a chance at writing or drawing?*

**MO:** Yeah. If I was to work with these characters, I would want to have a hand in the story, whether I was writing it myself, or just giving the outline to another writer. I would definitely want to work on Daredevil, obviously. Spider-Man, a little bit. I wouldn't want to do too much with Spider-Man, but I would definitely enjoy drawing him.

So, Daredevil, Spider-Man, Batman, Captain America. I think, actually, I would love to do a Captain America miniseries. I think I have a pretty good take on what I would like to do with him.

Thor I struggle with, because I don't know. [*laughter*] I just don't know about Thor. Sometimes I think I would definitely like to, other times I think that'd be redundant. [*general laughter*] And, off the top of my head, that would be it. I'm sure, if I was offered certain other things, I would do it as well.

I just did a Catwoman story for Secret Files, which was fun. Mainly I did it because I got to work with Ed Brubaker, who I like a lot. I was surprised that I got to draw Batman in there, so that was neat.

And Grendel. I did a Grendel story for *Grendel: Red, White, & Black*. And drawing Grendel was a lot of fun, too.

**BB:** *Yeah. That Matt Wagner kid, he's another one who might have a future in the funny book biz.*

**MO:** Yeah. I think he'll go places. [*general laughter*]

But that's almost it. I'm sure I could think of other things, but not a lot.

**BB:** *You mentioned that you had a good take on Cap. How do you see him?*

**MO:** Well, I see Captain America as fresh out of World War II. I think Marvel continuity says that nothing is older than nine years [in their current universe]. Bill, you're old enough to have known guys who were in 'Nam, even if you were a kid, and look how long it affected them. So imagine somebody from World War II, who's been through everything he's been through, and seen everything he's seen. And I'm not just talking about the atrocities, but the time period that he comes from. He's from a time period where whites and blacks were not treated equally. And, even if you were a complete liberal at that time of history, you'd still have a skewed view of race relations, whether it's your vernacular or just the shock that you'd have at people being treated equally. Not just black and white, but other cultures, and the sexes as well.

I would never make him a bigot, but I would love to deal with his naiveté of the culture, and how it's changed. I think it's a great way to see America as it is now, and as it was then. The fact that Captain America comes from a time, just talking about meaning and stories, he comes from a time when America had meaning. Even if it was a false meaning, it was a meaning. Now, America has no meaning. Our culture is pop culture. Our history goes back a whole couple of hundred years, but if you look at our national culture, we really have no traditions. Most of our traditions are regionalized.

You know, if you have a tradition of certain events and holidays, they all vary from place to place, and they're all very different. I don't think we really have a unified culture.

**BB:** *If we do, it's the commercial culture, and a very disposable one.*

**MO:** Exactly. Pop culture. And I think Captain America would be repulsed by that, frightened by it.

**BB:** *There were certain early aspects of it that he might have encountered way back in the day, but they were fairly benign. I'm thinking of things that presaged pop culture, like Uncle Sam and the Norman Rockwell strain of commercial art. And that's not even addressing the whole aspect of Future Shock he might encounter with the level and common nature of current technology.*

**MO:** Yeah. Yeah, I would just love to draw Captain America trying to play a game on a PlayStation. I remember I hadn't played video games in years, and it was in like the early '90s. The last time I had played video games was a Sega game. And somebody had one of these three-dimensional games, I forget which one, where you can go anywhere in the game. All of a sudden I felt like I was ninety! I didn't know how to control the thing, I didn't know where I was, and I was getting dizzy playing it and stuff.

I would just love to draw Captain America trying to play a video game. He wouldn't even know why you would play a video game. [*general laughter*]

**BB:** *Right, and you could have a really young kid, like of seven or eight, just kickin' his butt. [more laughter]*

**MO:** Yeah, really. And the shock he would have at playing some of these games.

**BB:** *And just the level of violence that they include, too.*

**MO:** Right. Captain America wouldn't be shocked by violence, but he would be shocked by how our generations now handle violence.

So I think there's a ton of stuff you could do with him. It would be a lot of fun.

**BB:** *What about the character of Daredevil intrigues you?*

**MO:** It's crime noir in a superhero outfit. It's gritty crime noir in a superhero outfit. That's what I love about it. So just do crime stories with him. That's how I see it.

Batman's noir, but he feels like a cleaner noir. And, even though you put him in costumes, I think the fact that Batman has these big ears and a cape, he seems like less realistic crime noir, if that makes any sense. Daredevil feels like a vigilante who maybe could actually exist. And he doesn't seem as capable as Batman, so it seems like Daredevil's in the gutter, with bloody knuckles. He's fighting on a real street level, really involved with what seems like day-to-day crime. Whereas Batman, I would think of him saving the city, versus saving the person on the street.

**BB:** *A bit like Mike Hammer versus Sherlock Holmes?*

**MO:** Yeah, exactly.

**BB:** *Well, a Sherlock Holmes crossed with Zorro.*

**MO:** Yeah. Yeah, you know, I think Batman's too close to James Bond.

**BB:** *Right, especially with the Bruce Wayne connection.*

**MO:** Yeah. The Bruce Wayne stuff I'm not interested in at all. I'm just interested in Batman. So my stories would be kinda limited. I think I would probably do stories that were very much in the vein of *The Spirit*, where the story would be about the crime and, in the end, the Spirit would show up and resolve it. It wasn't about the Spirit, it was about the things in the Spirit's world.

So with Batman, that's probably the type of stories I would like to do. Where we see the crimes from the criminals' point of view. And then Batman would be involved in it, but it wouldn't be about Batman.

Whereas Daredevil, I think, is much more hands on. He feels like he's the guy who's going to help you when you're getting mugged.

**BB:** *What about Spidey?*

**MO:** It's just the pure childhood fantasy, the unadulterated joy of Spider-Man. And he's fun to draw. It just goes back to when I was a kid and watching the Bakshi

cartoons, and my earliest comic book reading experiences were reading the Spider-Man run and laying up
at night thinking, "Gosh, why can't Peter Parker get a
break?" [*general laughter*]

In *Spider-Man*, I'm interested in both characters.
I'm interested in Peter Parker and in Spider-Man.
Same thing with Daredevil.

**BB:** *Why do you find those alter egos interesting, and not
the Batman's?*

**MO:** Well, I can't relate to Bruce Wayne is why. He's like a
schizophrenic rich guy who . . . Does he have a life?
Doesn't he? I mean, I know how hard it is to balance
my work life with my family. How could you be a
multimillionaire and run these invisible companies
that he supposedly has, that backs all this money that
he has like nothing to do with? I just don't understand
the whole Bruce Wayne thing.

But Spider-Man, all the clichés are true. All of
us are trying to get through our everyday life, and the
rejection of the teenager thing. Everything that Stan
Lee's ever said about Spider-Man is true. That's why
we all love Spider-Man.

Matt Murdock I find interesting because he's
blind, and he's a lawyer. It's that whole double entendre
thing of the lawyer/vigilante. His blindness and his

connection with the street-level crime, and the street-level people. I found it interesting that Hell's Kitchen doesn't really exist anymore. I don't know how much that's addressed in the comic anymore, but Hell's Kitchen used to be this great ghetto. But now it's turned. They've renovated it. It's not even Hell's Kitchen anymore. So I'd just be interested in the whole environment. There's a lot to Daredevil to explore, both in him, as Daredevil and as Matt Murdock, and in the environment.

And I would never do anything with Elektra. [*laughter*]

**BB:** *She doesn't interest you?*

**MO:** No, she's great but . . . Their love story was great, and it happened, and it's just wrong to bring it back. [*laughter*] You know what I mean? I'd do Elektra by herself. I think that's fine. But there's no way to do another great Elektra/Daredevil story, after it's already been done. Because it only lessens what was done before, and it lessens what you're trying to do now. I just hope that nobody I like is writing that story right now. [*general laughter*]

**BB:** *Do you feel that there's that much left for you to accomplish?*

**MO:** I'm hitting my peak at twenty-nine! It's all downhill from here! [*general laughter*] I'll get a lifetime achievement award when I'm thirty, then I'll be happy.

I'm not just doing this stuff for the wrong reasons, all these side projects and stuff. It's not that I'm overly ambitious, it's just that, honestly, I've had so much rejection and failure in my career, that in this time of success, I'm trying to build up a foundation for the future—so I can be around. I want to be like Frank Miller, not in the sense of the accolades and all that, although that'd all be great, but I want to work in this industry for the rest of my life, for as long as there is an industry. So I'm hoping that, by building this foundation of creations now, that will be stable for me in the future.

Maybe I'm still really paranoid, but when you've gone through as much rejection, and career low points, and failure as much as I have, and I know there's people who have been through much worse, that when you get to a high point now, you really appreciate it and you want to do everything you can to sustain it, and take care of it, and not blow it. [*laughter*]

**BB:** *What do you get from doing the work, personally— aside from that immense paycheck, of course?*

**MO:** I haven't seen that one yet, because every time I do see it coming, the tax man comes and takes about half of it. [*general laughter*] Really what I get is . . . I guess it's pretty sad, and I think a lot of artists are the same way. I'm a very happy person now, I'm playing the violins for myself, but I grew up unhappy. And I spent a lot of time daydreaming about being some place else other than where I was, about escaping. And that created in my mind, even when I became happy, and became satisfied with life itself, I had gone through that for such a long period of time that it created a pattern in my mind to want to escape, and to want to think about other places and other realms and stuff, whether I needed to or not. Whereas early on I needed to, so I was always escaping in my mind to these other places, it became a habit.

So that's why like now, I don't live in an area where there's other comic book artists. Neil lives around me, that's it, and I see Neil from time to time. But I don't have people saying, like if I lived in Portland or maybe New York where there's a comic book community of people, of people who say, "Oh, wow, the latest issue was great!" When *Powers* was first coming out, and people were going crazy over it, I didn't really believe it because I wasn't seeing any of that. I was reading about it on the Internet, but that didn't seem real to me. It wasn't until I went to my first convention after *Powers* came out, in Baltimore, and I had my first line of people that I realized, "Wow, people actually like this."

So it's not an ego thing. It's not the kind of thing where I put out a new book and then I can't wait for everybody to tell me how great it was. Because, nine times out of ten, I don't know how people are reacting. Or, if I do know, I don't believe it. Because reading it online is completely different than having somebody actually tell you that stuff. So I honestly don't think it's for ego reasons.

I think it's still I just love to escape in my own mind. And that's why I love *Powers* and *Hammer* so much, because that's what I do.

**BB:** *What do you hope that your readers get from you work?*

**MO:**  The same thing. I hope that, for a couple of minutes a day, they connect and believe in this little world that we've set ourselves up in *Powers* and *Hammer*. Find themselves there, and find themselves shocked and afraid when they're reading *Powers*, and amazed and swept away when they're reading *Hammer*. Just for a couple of minutes.

## Selected *Works*

Michael Avon Oeming has, over the past decade and a half, produced a surprising and truly diverse amount of art and scripts for comics, original graphic novels, and illustrated books, as well as independent films. Therefore, the list below is by no means comprehensive. Instead, it concentrates on his most popular and unique work, both as an illustrator and author, all of which should be readily available via book stores, comic shops, and libraries.

## Collections, Illustrated Books, and Graphic Novels Intended for All Ages

Berman, Dan, and Michael Avon Oeming. *Stormbreaker: The Saga of Beta Ray Bill*. Illustrated by Andrea Di Vito. New York, NY: Marvel Comics, 2005.

Carey, Mike, and Michael Avon Oeming. *Red Sonja: She-Devil with a Sword Vol. 1*. Runnemede, NJ: Dynamite Entertainment, 2006.

Glass, Brian, and Michael Avon Oeming. *Quixote Novel.* Illustrated by Michael Avon Oeming. Berkeley, CA: Image Comics, 2005.

Gross, Allan. *Dr. Cyborg.* Illustrated by Michael Avon Oeming, Adrian Salmon, and Neil Vokes. Berkeley, CA: Image Comics, 2004.

Gunter, Miles, and Michael Avon Oeming. *Bastard Samurai Vol. 1: Samurai Noir.* Illustrated by Miles Gunter and Michael Avon Oeming. Berkeley, CA: Image Comics, 2007.

Jones, R. A., and Brett Lewis. *Bulletproof Monk.* Illustrated by Michael Avon Oeming. Berkeley, CA: Image Comics, 2002.

Krueger, Jim. *The Footsoldiers.* Illustrated by Michael Avon Oeming. San Francisco, CA: AiT/PlanetLar, 2001

Oeming, Michael Avon. *Ares: God of War.* Illustrated by Travel Foreman. New York, NY: Marvel Comics, 2006.

Oeming, Michael Avon. *Avengers Disassembled: Thor.* Illustrated by Andrea Di Vito. New York, NY: Marvel Comics, 2004.

Oeming, Michael Avon. *Red Sonja: She-Devil with a Sword Vol. 2: Arrowsmiths.* Runnemede, NJ: Dynamite Entertainment, 2006.

Oeming, Michael Avon. *Thor: Blood Oath.* Illustrated by Scott Kolins. New York, NY: Marvel Comics, 2007.

Oeming, Michael Avon. *Wings of Anansi.* Illustrated by Greg Titus. Berkeley, CA: Image Comics, 2005.

Oeming, Michael Avon, and Mark Wheatley. *Hammer of the Gods Vol. 1: Mortal Enemy*. Berkeley, CA: Image Comics, 2002.

Oeming, Michael Avon, and Mark Wheatley. *Hammer of the Gods Vol. 2: Back from the Dead*. Berkeley, CA: Image Comics, 2005.

## Graphic Novels and Collections Intended for Teens and Older Readers

Bendis, Brian Michael. *Powers: The Definitive Collection Vol. 1*. Illustrated by Michael Avon Oeming. New York, NY: Marvel Comics, 2005.

Bendis, Brian Michael. *Powers: The Definitive Collection Vol. 2*. Illustrated by Michael Avon Oeming. New York, NY: Marvel Comics, 2007.

Bendis, Brian Michael. *Powers: Script Book*. Illustrated by Michael Avon Oeming. Berkeley, CA: Image Comics, 2001.

Bendis, Brian Michael. *Powers Vol. 1: Who Killed Retro Girl?* Illustrated by Michael Avon Oeming. Berkeley, CA: Image Comics, 2006.

Bendis, Brian Michael. *Powers Vol. 2: Roleplay*. Illustrated by Michael Avon Oeming. Berkeley, CA: Image Comics, 2001.

Bendis, Brian Michael. *Powers Vol. 3: Little Deaths*. Illustrated by Michael Avon Oeming. Berkeley, CA: Image Comics, 2006.

Bendis, Brian Michael. *Powers Vol. 4: Supergroup*.
Illustrated by Michael Avon Oeming. Berkeley, CA:
Image Comics, 2006.

Bendis, Brian Michael. *Powers Vol. 5: Anarchy*. Illustrated
by Michael Avon Oeming. Berkeley, CA: Image
Comics, 2003.

Bendis, Brian Michael. *Powers Vol. 6: Sellouts*. Illustrated
by Michael Avon Oeming. New York, NY: Marvel
Comics, 2004.

Bendis, Brian Michael. *Powers Vol. 7: Forever*. Illustrated
by Michael Avon Oeming. New York, NY: Marvel
Comics, 2004.

Bendis, Brian Michael. *Powers Vol. 8: Legends*. Illustrated
by Michael Avon Oeming. New York, NY: Marvel
Comics, 2005.

Bendis, Brian Michael. *Powers Vol. 9: Psychotic*. Illustrated
by Michael Avon Oeming. New York, NY: Marvel
Comics, 2006.

Bendis, Brian Michael. *Powers Vol. 10: Cosmic*. Illustrated
by Michael Avon Oeming. New York, NY: Marvel
Comics, 2007.

Bendis, Brian Michael. *Powers Vol. 11: Secret Identity*.
Illustrated by Michael Avon Oeming. New York, NY:
Marvel Comics, 2007.

Berman, Dan, and Michael Avon Oeming. *Blood River*.
Illustrated by Brian Quinn. Berkeley, CA: Image
Comics, 2005.

Berman, Dan, and Michael Avon Oeming. *Six*. Illustrated by Ethan Beavers. Berkeley, CA: Image Comics, 2004.

Glass, Brian, and Michael Avon Oeming. *86 Voltz: The Dead Girl*. Illustrated by Robert Hack and Michael Avon Oeming. Berkeley, CA: Image Comics, 2005

Oeming, Michael Avon. *The Cross Bronx Vol. 1*. Illustrated by Ivan Brandon. Berkeley, CA: Image Comics, 2007.

Oeming, Michael Avon. *Parliament of Justice*. Illustrated by Neil Vokes. Berkeley, CA: Image Comics, 2003.

Smith, Kevin. *Bluntman and Chronic*. Illustrated by Michael Allred and Michael Avon Oeming. Berkeley, CA: Image Comics, 2001.

Wagner, Matt. *Grendel: Red, White, & Black*. Illustrated by Phil Noto, Michael Avon Oeming, Jill Thompson, and various. Milwaukie, OR: Dark Horse, 2005.

# Selected Awards

Despite being an incredibly prolific and increasingly popular creator of comics, Michael Avon Oeming has so far won only one award. However, it seems only a matter of time before newly bestowed honors will be joining the trophy Mike has won to date.

**Will Eisner Comic Industry Awards for Achievement in Comic Books**
2001
Best New Series for *Powers*

# Glossary

**amalgamation** A combination of two or more different things into one unified whole.

**analogous** Showing a likeness or similarity, allowing an analogy to be drawn.

**anarchic** Lacking order, regularity, or control

**arc** The continuous progression or line of development in a story.

**avant-garde** Artistically new, experimental, or unconventional.

**benign** Neutral or harmless in its effect or influence.

**bigot** Someone who has very strong opinions and views, especially on matters of politics, religion, or ethnicity, and refuses to accept other views.

**circumvent** To manage to get around something, especially by resourcefulness.

**cleric** A member of the clergy.

**cliché** Something, such as an expression or phrase, that has become overly common or familiar.

**codex** A collection of ancient manuscripts, especially of classics or Scripture.

**desolate**  Bare, deserted, and uninhabited.

**detriment**  Damage, harm, or disadvantage.

**double entendre**  A word or expression capable of two interpretations, one of which is usually risqué.

**efficiency apartment**  A small, usually furnished one-room apartment with minimal kitchen and bathroom facilities.

**esoteric**  Difficult to understand.

**exposition**  Part of a literary or dramatic work in which the basic facts of character and setting are made known.

**flagship**  The most important or finest among a group of similar and related things.

**foreshadowing**  Representing, indicating, or suggesting something before it happens.

**fruition**  The point in which something has a desired outcome.

**genesis**  The origin of something.

**German Expressionism**  An artistic movement in post-WWI Germany that influenced many disciplines, including theater, painting, sculpture, and film. Films in particular sought to give shape to psychological states through stylized visuals—using sharply exaggerated shadows and high-contrast lighting, as well as skewed set design and unusual camera angles.

**gestate**  To conceive of and gradually develop in the mind.

**Hell's Kitchen**  A New York City neighborhood once known for its crime and corruption.

**iconic**  Relating to or characteristic of somebody or something admired.

**monotonous**  Tediously uniform, repetitive, or unvarying.

**noir**  Crime fiction featuring cynical characters and bleak settings and outlook. Also known as film noir, these films were often filmed in urban surroundings with extensive use of shadows and featuring antiheroes.

**Norse**  Norwegian or Scandinavian.

**parody**  A piece of writing or music that deliberately closely imitates another work in a comic or satirical way.

**presaged**  Predicted a future event; foreshadowed.

**renaissance**  Rebirth; a period of vigorous artistic activity.

**Rosetta stone**  A stone tablet found in 1799 that contained the same text repeated in Egyptian hieroglyphics, Egyptian demotic script, and Greek, thereby supplying the first clue to deciphering Egyptian hieroglyphics.

**simpatico**  Being on the same wavelength.

**surmount**  To overcome.

**thumbnails**  Concise, miniature sketches.

**unadulterated**  Pure.

**vernacular**  Relating to or characteristic of a place, group, or period.

**vigilante**  A self-appointed doer of justice; someone who punishes lawbreakers personally and illegally rather than relying on authorized officials.

# For More Information

## AiT/Planet Lar
2034 47th Avenue
San Francisco, CA 94116
Web site: http://www.ait-planetlar.com

## Dark Horse Comics
10956 SE Main Street
Milwaukie, OR 97222
(503) 652-8815
Web site: http://www.darkhorse.com

## Dynamic Forces
155 East 9th Avenue, Suite B
Runnemede, NJ 08078-1158
(856) 312-1040
Web site: http://www.dynamicforces.com

## Image Comics
1942 University Avenue, Suite 305

Berkeley, CA 94704

Web site: http://www.imagecomics.com

**Insight Studios Group**

P.O. Box 685

Westminster, MD 21158

Web site: http://www.insightstudiosgroup.com

**Marvel Entertainment, Inc.**

417 5th Avenue

New York, NY 10016

(212) 576-4000

Web site: http://www.marvel.com

# Web Sites

Due to the changing nature of Internet links, Rosen Publishing has developed an online list of Web sites related to the subject of this book. This site is updated regularly. Please use this link to access the list:

http://www.rosenlinks.com/twgn/mioe

# For Further Reading

Barron, Mike, and Steve Rude. *Nexus, Vol. 1*. Milwaukie, OR: Dark Horse Books, 2005.

Barron, Mike, and Steve Rude. *Nexus, Vol. 2*. Milwaukie, OR: Dark Horse Books, 2006.

Barron, Mike, and Steve Rude. *Nexus, Vol. 3*. Milwaukie, OR: Dark Horse Books, 2006.

Barron, Mike, and Steve Rude. *Nexus, Vol. 4*. Milwaukie, OR: Dark Horse Books, 2006.

Barron, Mike, and Steve Rude. *Nexus, Vol. 5*. Milwaukie, OR: Dark Horse Books, 2007.

Bendis, Brian Michael. *Jinx*. Berkeley, CA: Image Comics, 2001.

Bendis, Brian Michael, and Marc Andreyko. *Torso: A True Crime Graphic Novel*. Berkeley, CA: Image Comics, 2001.

Eisner, Will. *Comics and Sequential Art: Principles & Practice of the World's Most Popular Art Form*. Tamarac, FL: Poorhouse Press, 1994.

Eisner, Will. *Graphic Storytelling and Visual Narrative.* Tamarac, FL: Poorhouse Press, 1996.

Eisner, Will. *Will Eisner's New York: Life in the Big City.* New York, NY: W. W. Norton, 2006.

Khoury, George, and Eric Nolen-Weathington. *Modern Masters Volume Six: Arthur Adams.* Raleigh, NC: TwoMorrows Publishing, 2006.

King, Stephen. *On Writing: A Memoir of the Craft.* New York, NY: Scribner, 2000.

McKee, Robert. *Story: Substance, Structure, Style, and the Principles of Screenwriting.* New York, NY: ReganBooks, 1997.

# Index

# Acknowledgments

Bill Baker would like to take a moment to thank . . .
First and foremost, Mike Oeming, for his continued and
enthusiastic support of my work, and for simply saying,
"Yes!" Without that kindness, my friend, this book would
never have happened.

All the good folks at Rosen Books, especially
Kristin Eck, Iris Rosoff, and Elizabeth Gavril, who have
provided valuable guidance and insightful commentary
while seeing this book to press; Nicholas Rook and his
team for their fine design work; and Roger Rosen, who
brought me into the fold.

Finally, you, the reader, for picking up this volume
and making it all real once again, if only for a fleeting
moment. You've all helped make this an entirely pleasurable

and truly rewarding experience. I am indebted to each and every one of you, in ways both large and small.

Thank you
BB

## About the Interviewer

Over the course of the past decade, veteran comics journalist Bill Baker has contributed interviews and feature stories, reviews, and news reportage to various magazines, including *Cinefantastique/CFQ*, *Comic Book Marketplace*, *International Studio*, *Sketch,* and *Tripwire.* During that same period, Bill also served as an interviewer and reporter for a number of Web sites, including www.ComicBookResources.com and www.WizardWorld.com. These days, when he's not working on his latest interview book, Bill serves as the host of "Baker's Dozen" for www.WorldFamousComics.com.

Bill currently lives and works in the wilds of the Upper Peninsula of Michigan, for some unknown and quite likely complicated reason. You can learn more about Bill's activities, past and present, by visiting his blog at http://specfric.blogspot.com and his professional Web site at www.BloodintheGutters.com.

## About the Interviewee

Michael Avon Oeming broke into comics at the age of fourteen, working as an inker for Marvel Comics. He very soon found himself penciling *Judge Dredd* for DC Comics. After that, he completely reinvented his style and approach to making art, resulting in his involvement in a variety of creator-owned properties, including the critically acclaimed *Hammer of the Gods* and the award-winning *Powers*. More recently, in addition to his ongoing duties drawing *Powers*, he has begun to write scripts for various titles published by Marvel and Dynamite Entertainment, as well as for a variety of new creator-owned projects. Oeming currently lives in New Jersey, where he often has way too much fun for his own good while doing what he loves most: creating comics and independent films, and spending time with his family.

**Series Design:** Les Kanturek